VIKKI L. PENDLETON

KNOWLEDGE NUGGETS

First published by FeelizePublishingHouse 2024

Copyright © 2024 by Vikki L. Pendleton

All rights reserved. No part of this publication may be reproduced, stored or transmitted in any form or by any means, electronic, mechanical, photocopying, recording, scanning, or otherwise without written permission from the publisher. It is illegal to copy this book, post it to a website, or distribute it by any other means without permission.

First edition

This book was professionally typeset on Reedsy.
Find out more at reedsy.com

Contents

Introduction   1

CHAPTER 1   3

    RELATIONSHIPS   3

CHAPTER 2   5

CHAPTER 3   8

CHAPTER 4   10

CHAPTER 5   13

CHAPTER 6   15

CHAPTER 7   16

CHAPTER 8   17

CHAPTER 9   18

CHAPTER 10   19

CHAPTER 11   20

CHAPTER 12   21

CHAPTER 13   23

CHAPTER 14   25

CHAPTER 15   27

CHAPTER 16   29

CHAPTER 17   31

    SELF   31

CHAPTER 18   32

CHAPTER 19   36

CHAPTER 20   38

CHAPTER 21   40

CHAPTER 22   42

CHAPTER 23   44

CHAPTER 24   46

CHAPTER 25   48

CHAPTER 26   50

CHAPTER 27   53

CHAPTER 28   55

CHAPTER 29   57

CHAPTER 30   59

CHAPTER 31   60

CHAPTER 32   62

CHAPTER 33   64

CHAPTER 34   68

CHAPTER 35   70

CHAPTER 36   72

CHAPTER 37   74

CHAPTER 38   76

CHAPTER 39   78

CHAPTER 40   80

CHAPTER 41   82

CHAPTER 42   84

CHAPTER 43   87

CHAPTER 44   89

   LOVE   89

CHAPTER 45   94

CHAPTER 46   96

CHAPTER 47   97

CHAPTER 48   99

CHAPTER 49   101

CHAPTER 50   103

CHAPTER 51   104

CHAPTER 52   106

CHAPTER 53   108

CHAPTER 54   110

CHAPTER 55   112

CHAPTER 56   114

CHAPTER 57   116

CHAPTER 58   118

CHAPTER 59   120

CHAPTER 60   122

CHAPTER 61   124

CHAPTER 62   126

   LEADERSHIP   126

Also by Vikki L. Pendleton   127

Introduction

INTRODUCTION

Within these pages are words of wisdom straight from my heart. It is my prayer that these words of wisdom will transcend time and speak to the heart of all humanity.

With a special love it is my purpose to guide, help, and aid in the progression of the life path others choose to take.

My legal name is Vikki LeTonya Pendleton. My nickname is Sugar. I am a Christian Hip Hop artist and Christian stage DJ for concerts and Christian events that have performers. Please listen to my music on any listening format. You can find it under my artist's name DJ JChill or DJ JCHILL. (Some formats are case sensitive).

JCHILL is an acronym for Jesus Christ Has Infinite Lasting Love.

Once this book hits the market, I will be offering services for Power Couple Contracts, Matrimony Contracts, Consultations to help you find your Divine Purpose, Consultations on developing into becoming a Chosen vessel, specifically tailored Daily Affirmations for you, Speaking engagements, conferences, conventions, book signings, music performances, concerts, and Stage DJ formats.

In the quiet moments of reflection, amidst the noise of this sometimes-chaotic world, I found solace in words that stirred my soul and illuminated my path. And this collection of my own words of wisdom, born from my own experiences and reflections, offers a glimpse into the insights that have shaped and guided my very own life. May these words resonate with you, bring clarity to your thoughts, and offer a guiding light on your own journey of self-discovery.

It is a necessity for God's chosen vessels to always increase in wisdom and knowledge because this is how we lead others effectively. Prayerfully this book of Knowledge Nuggets will aid in your leadership and personal development as well as your life journey.

   With Love,

   Vikki L. Pendleton

CHAPTER 1

RELATIONSHIPS

"Do not continue to withhold good from the individual deserving this of you."

Continuing to withhold good from someone who deserves it can have detrimental consequences on both the individual and your relationship with them.

1. **The individual may feel hurt and rejected:** If someone is deserving of something positive or kind from you but you continue to withhold it, they may feel hurt, rejected, and unappreciated. This can damage their self-esteem and lead to feelings of resentment towards you.

2. **The relationship may suffer**: Withholding good from someone who deserves it can strain your relationship with that person. It can create a barrier between you and make it difficult to connect on a deeper level. Over time, this can lead to distance, misunderstandings, and conflict.

3. **Negative impact on your reputation**: When you consistently withhold good from someone who deserves it, it can reflect poorly of you are as a person. Others may view you as selfish, unkind, or unreliable, which can harm your reputation and relationships with others.

4. **Missed opportunities for growth and connection**: By withholding good from someone who deserves it, you may be missing out on opportunities for personal growth and deepening your relationship with that person. Showing kindness, generosity, and appreciation can lead to positive experiences and strengthen your bond with others.

In conclusion, continuing to withhold good from someone who deserves it can have serious consequences on both the individual and your relationship with them. It's important to reflect on your actions and consider the impact it may have on others before choosing to withhold good from someone deserving of it.

CHAPTER 2

"Be an advocate for the unfortunate and the defenseless."

Being an advocate for the unfortunate and defenseless is a noble and impactful way to make a difference in the world. Here are some steps you can take to effectively advocate for those who are marginalized, oppressed, or in need:

1. **Educate yourself**: Always take the time to educate yourself about the issues facing the unfortunate and defenseless, such as poverty, discrimination, injustice, and human rights violations. Learn about the root causes of these issues, their impact on individuals and communities, and the ways in which you can make a difference.

2. **Raise awareness**: Use your gifts, talents, and vocal platform to raise awareness about the challenges and struggles faced by the marginalized and defenseless. Share information, stories, and statistics on social media, in conversations with friends and family, and in your community to shine a light on these important issues.

3. **Support and volunteer**: Get involved with organizations, charities, and initiatives that support the unfortunate and defenseless. Volunteer your time, skills, and resources to help those in need, and donate to causes that are working to address social injustices and improve the lives of vulnerable populations.

4. **Advocate for policy change**: Get involved in efforts to push for policy change at the local, national, and global levels that will benefit and advocate for others. Write to your elected officials, participate in

advocacy campaigns, and join pressing movements that are working to address systemic injustices and promote social change.

5. **Stand up against injustice**: Speak out and take action when you witness discrimination, oppression, or injustice in your community or workplace. Be an ally and advocate for those who are marginalized, oppressed, or silenced, and use your privilege and influence to amplify their voices and support their struggles.

6. **Practice empathy and compassion:** Approach your advocacy work with empathy, compassion and a willingness to listen and learn from those who are directly impacted by the issues you are advocating for. Show respect, understanding, and solidarity Ritchie with the unfortunate and defenseless, and strive to be an ally and supporter in their fight for justice and equality.

By taking these steps and actively advocating for the unfortunate and defenseless, you can contribute to positive social change, promote justice and equality, and make a meaningful difference in the lives of those who are most in need of support in solidarity.

The Bible places a strong emphasis on advocating for the unfortunate and defenseless, and it contains many verses that speak to the importance of caring for the marginalized, oppressed, and vulnerable members of society. Here are a few examples of Bible verses that highlight the call to advocate for those in need:

1. **Proverbs 31:8-9**: "Speak up for those who cannot speak for themselves, for the rights of all who are destitute. Speak up for them and judge them fairly; Always defend the rights of the poor and needy."

2. **Isaiah 1:17**: "Practice doing right; Always seek justice. Defend the oppressed. Take up the cause of the fatherless; Plead the case of the widow."

3. **Micah 6:8:** "God has shown you, and all others, what is good. And what does God require from you? To be just and to love mercy and to walk

humbly with your Heavenly Father."

4. **Matthew 25:35-40**: "When I was hungry, you gave me food to eat. When I was thirsty, you gave me something to drink. I was a stranger to you, yet you invited me into your home. When I was naked, you gave me clothing to wear. When I was sick, you took care of me. When I was in prison, you visited me. Then the righteous ones replied, 'Lord when did we ever see you hungry, and when did we give you food to eat? When were you thirsty Lord, and we gave you something to drink? When were you a stranger to us and we showed you hospitality? When were you naked and we gave you clothing? When did we ever see you sick or see you in prison and visited you there?' And the Lord God answered them saying, I assure you, when you did this for one of the least of your brothers or sisters, you were doing it for me!" In this passage, Jesus talks about the importance of caring for the hungry, thirsty, stranger, naked, sick, and imprisoned, emphasizing that when we care for these individuals, we are also caring for Him.

5. **Galatians 6:2**: "You are to help carry the burdens and problems of others, and when you do this you are obeying the law of Christ why do you think you feel sad honey."

These verses and others in the bible underscore the Christian responsibility to advocate for social justice, defend the rights of the vulnerable, and show compassion and love for those in need. By following these teachings and actively advocating for the unfortunate and defenseless, Christians are living out their faith and fulfilling God's call to love and care for others.

CHAPTER 3

"You will be rewarded for being kind to those who wrong you."

Being kind to those who wrong you can be a challenging and emotionally taxing experience, but it is an admirable and courageous choice. While there may not always be immediate or tangible rewards for your kindness, there are several potential benefits and positive outcomes that can result from your actions:

1. **Inner peace and personal growth**: Choosing kindness and forgiveness in the face of adversity can lead to a sense of inner peace and emotional healing period by letting go of anger and resentment, you can free yourself from negative emotions and cultivate a sense of empathy, compassion, and personal growth.
2. **Building positive relationships**: Your acts of kindness and forgiveness can have a positive impact on your relationships with others. Showing grace and understanding to those who wrong you can strengthen trust, foster mutual respect, and encourage a sense of empathy and goodwill in your interactions with others.
3. **Setting an example**: By choosing to respond with kindness and forgiveness, even in difficult situations, you can inspire others to follow your example and cultivate a culture of compassion, understanding, and forgiveness in your community or social circle.
4. **Redirecting negative energy**: Responding to wrongdoing with kindness

can help break the cycle of negativity and conflict and redirect negative energy towards more positive and constructive outcomes. Your acts of kindness can promote healing, reconciliation, and understanding, and contribute to a more peaceful and harmonious environment.

5. **Personal integrity and character**: Choosing kindness and forgiveness in the face of adversity demonstrates strength of character, integrity, and emotional maturity. Your actions can reflect your values, beliefs, and principles, and showcase your ability to rise above challenges and adversities with grace and compassion.

It's important to remember that while being kind and forgiving to those who have wronged you may not always result in immediate rewards or acknowledgement, the positive impact of your actions can have far-reaching and long-lasting effects on yourself and others. Your kindness and compassion have the power to create positive change, foster healing and understanding, and contribute to a more harmonious and interconnected world.

CHAPTER 4

"A friend loves at all times."

A true friend can show love at all times through various actions and behaviors. Here are some ways a friend can demonstrate love consistently:

1. **Supporting you**: A friend who loves you will always be there to offer support, encouragement, and a listening ear. They will stand by you through both good times and

bad, providing comfort and reassurance when needed.

1. **Being reliable**: A loving friend will be reliable and trustworthy. They will keep their promises, show up when they say they will, and be someone you can always count on.
2. **Showing appreciation**: A friend who loves you will express gratitude for your friendship and show appreciation for who you are. They will make an effort to acknowledge your strengths, qualities, and the positive impact you have on their life.
3. **Respecting boundaries**: A loving friend respects your boundaries, both emotiona and physical. They will not pressure you into doing things you are uncomfortable with and will always consider your feelings and needs.
4. **Celebrating your successes**: A friend who loves you will genuinely celebrate your accomplishments, milestones, and successes. They will be happy for your achievements and support you in reaching your goals.

5. **Offering constructive feedback**: A loving friend will provide constructive feedback and guidance when needed. They will offer honest advice and help you grow and improve as a person.

6. **Forgiving and understanding**: A loving friend will be forgiving and understanding when conflicts or misunderstandings arise. They will be willing to work through disagreements and conflicts, showing patience, empathy, and compassion.

Overall, a friend who loves you will consistently demonstrate care, support, respect, and understanding. They will be a positive influence in your life, fostering a strong and healthy friendship built on mutual love and respect.

Your showing love to a friend at all times involves consistently demonstrating care, support, and appreciation for them. Here are some ways you can show love to a friend:

1. **Be there for them**: Show your friend that you are there for them and available to offer support, a listening ear, and encouragement when they need it. Make time to be present in their life and show genuine interest in their well-being.

2. **Communicate openly and honestly**: Maintain open and honest communication with your friend. Share your thoughts, feelings, and experiences with them, and listen attentively when they do the same. Communication is key to building a strong and supportive friendship.

3. **Show appreciation**: Express gratitude for your friend and the positive impact they have on your life. Let them know how much you value their friendship and what they mean to you. Small gestures of appreciation such as sending a thoughtful message or giving a heartfelt compliment, can go a long way.

4. **Celebrate their successes**: Acknowledge and celebrate your friends' accomplishments, milestones, and successes. Show genuine happiness for them and congratulate them on their achievements. Your support and encouragement will strengthen your bond and show that you care about their well-being.

5. **Respect their boundaries:** Respect your friends' boundaries and autonomy. Avoid pressuring them into doing things they are uncomfortable with and always consider their feelings and needs. Respect is a fundamental aspect of a healthy and loving friendship.

6. **Be forgiving and understanding**: Be willing to forgive and understand your friend when conflicts or misunderstandings arise. Approach disagreements with empathy and patience and work together to resolve conflicts in a respectful and constructive manner.

7. **Be loyal and trustworthy**: demonstrate loyalty and trustworthiness in your friendship by keeping your promises, being reliable, and standing by your friend through thick and thin. Show that you are a dependable and supportive presence in their life.

Overall, showing love to a friend at all times involves being present, communicative, supportive, and respectful. Be consistently demonstrating care, understanding, and appreciation for your friend, you can nurture a strong and enduring friendship built on love and mutual respect.

CHAPTER 5

"Forgive the offense. You will seek forgiveness when you offend as well."

Forgiving those who have offended you is beneficial for several reasons, even if seeking forgiveness when you have offended others.

1. **Cultivates Compassion**: Forgiving others can help you develop empathy and understanding, leading to a more compassionate and empathetic outlook. This can make you more likely to seek forgiveness when you have hurt someone, as you will be able to empathize with their feelings and understand the importance of asking for forgiveness.
2. **Promotes Emotional Healing**: Forgiveness can contribute to emotional healing and inner peace. Holding onto grudges and unresolved anger can be detrimental to your mental and emotional well-being. By forgiving those who have hurt you, you release yourself from negative emotions and find closure, which can make it easier for you to seek forgiveness when you have caused harm to others.
3. **Strengthens Relationships**: Forgiveness is essential for maintaining healthy relationships. By being willing to forgive others, you are fostering understanding, trust, and respect in your relationships. This can create a more supportive and compassionate environment where forgiveness is more readily given and sought when needed.
4. **Encourages Self-Reflection**: Forgiving others can also encourage self-reflection and personal growth. It can prompt you to evaluate your own actions and behavior, leading to increased self-awareness and a greater

willingness to seek forgiveness when necessary.

In summary, forgiving those who have offended you can have positive effects on your own emotional well-being, relationships, and personal growth. By cultivating a mindset of forgiveness, you are more likely to be empathetic and understanding towards others, including when seeking forgiveness for your own mistakes and offenses.

CHAPTER 6

"Give to the needy. It brings honor to do so."

Giving to the needy can bring honor to oneself in several ways. Firstly, it demonstrates compassion, empathy, and generosity, qualities that are highly valued in society. By showing kindness and support to those in need, an individual can earn respect and admiration from others for their selflessness and willingness to help those who are less fortunate.

Moreover, given to the needy can also create a sense of fulfillment and personal satisfaction. Knowing that you made a positive impact on someone's life, even in a small way, can bring a sense of joy and fulfillment that is deeply rewarding. This sense of fulfillment can boost self-esteem and confidence, leading to a stronger sense of self-worth and honor.

Additionally, acts of giving can inspire others to do the same, creating a ripple effect of kindness and generosity. By setting an example of generosity and compassion, individuals can inspire others to follow suit and contribute to making the world a better place for those in need. This can further enhance one's reputation and honor in the eyes of others.

In conclusion, given to the needy can bring honor to oneself by earning respect and admiration from others, fostering a sense of personal fulfillment, and inspiring positive change in the community. It is a noble and honorable act that can have a lasting impact on both the giver and those who are in need.

CHAPTER 7

"Companionship of foolish people will bring harm."

Companionship with foolish people can bring harm in various ways. Firstly, being around foolish individuals may lead to engaging in destructive behaviors or making poor decisions. Foolish people may not consider the consequences of their actions, and being influenced by them can lead to negative outcomes. Additionally foolish companions may not offer sound advice or support, leading to further harm or misjudgments.

Furthermore, associated with foolish people can also impact one's reputation and credibility. Others may judge a person based on the company they keep, and being associated with individuals who exhibit foolish behavior can reflect poorly on one's own character. This can lead to missed opportunities, damaged relationships, and a tarnished reputation.

In essence, companionship with foolish people can bring harm by affluence of one's actions, choices, and reputation in a negative way. It is important to surround yourself with individuals who uplift, support, and inspire personal growth rather than leading one down a destructive path.

CHAPTER 8

"Those quick to bring bad news will fall unto hardship. The lips that speak kindness and goodness brings life."

Those who are quick to bring bad news may find themselves facing hardship because spreading negativity can lead to a cycle of negativity in their own lives. It can also cause others to distance themselves from them and diminish their support network. On the other hand, those who speak kindness and goodness are more likely to attract positive energy and build strong, supportive relationships. Their words can bring life by uplifting and inspiring others, creating a ripple effect of goodwill and positivity. In the long run, speaking words of kindness and goodness will lead to a more fulfilling and harmonious life.

Proverbs 16:24

"Kind words are like honey—sweet to the soul and healthy for the body."

CHAPTER 9

"Do not keep low vibrational company or you will remain in a low place."

When you surround yourself with people who have low vibrational energy, such as negativity, pessimism, and toxic behaviors, their energy can affect your own vibration. This can lead to you absorbing their negative energy and thus keeping you in a low place emotionally and mentally.

Similarly, being around positive and high vibrational individuals can have the opposite effect, lifting you up and helping you maintain a higher vibrational state. It is important to be mindful of the energy and attitudes of the people you choose to surround yourself with, as they can greatly impact their own energy and overall well-being.

Corinthians 15:33: "Do not allow yourself to be misled: Entertaining bad company will corrupt your good character." This verse emphasizes the idea that the people you associate with can have an impact on your thoughts, attitudes, and behaviors.

Additionally, Proverbs 13:20 advises: "Walk with the wise and become wise, for a companion of fools suffers harm." This verse urges individuals to seek out wise and positive influences, as being around foolish or negative people can lead to harm.

While the Bible may not explicitly mention low vibrational energy, it does stress the importance of surrounding oneself with positive and uplifting influences in order to maintain a healthy and righteous lifestyle.

CHAPTER 10

"Give compliments more often to those around you."

Giving compliments regularly has several benefits:

1. **Boosts self-esteem**: Compliments make people feel valued and appreciated, boosting their self-esteem and confidence.
2. **Strengthens relationships**: Compliments foster positive relationships by creating a sense of connection and goodwill between individuals.
3. **Motivates and encourages**: Genuine compliments can motivate people to continue their efforts and achieve their goals by providing recognition for their accomplishments.
4. **Improves mood**: Receiving compliments can instantly uplift someone's mood and brighten their day, leading to increased happiness and positivity.
5. **Fosters a positive environment**: In environments where compliments are given freely, there tends to be a more positive atmosphere, where people feel supported and encouraged to succeed.

Overall, giving compliments is a simple yet powerful way to spread kindness and positivity, making the world a better place one compliment at a time.

CHAPTER 11

"Give without boasting and you will be rewarded openly."

The Bible teaches the importance of giving without boasting or seeking recognition for our actions. In Matthew 6:1- 4, Jesus instructs his disciples on the principles of giving, emphasizing the importance of doing so with a humble and sincere heart. Verse 4 specifically states, "so that your giving may be in secret. Then your father who sees what is done in secret, will reward you openly.

This passage suggests that when we give without seeking attention or praise from others, but rather out of a genuine desire to help and bless others, God will reward us openly. This reward may not necessarily be material or visible to others, but it can come in the form of God's blessings, peace, and fulfillment and knowing that we have done something good for someone in need.

The idea is that when we give with a pure heart, our motives are aligned with God's will, and He sees and acknowledges our generosity. Our reward may not come in the form of worldly recognition, but the spiritual rewards of peace, joy, and the favor of God are often far greater than any recognition we could receive from others.

In summary, the Bible teaches that true giving should be done with humility and sincerity, without seeking attention or praise from others. When we give in this way God sees our actions and rewards us openly in His own timing and according to His will.

CHAPTER 12

"The use of hateful words and actions will always return to its owner."

In the Bible, there are several verses that address the concept that hateful words and actions can ultimately return to the person who speaks or engages in them. This idea is often referred to as the principle of sowing and reaping, which means that the consequences of our actions will eventually come back to us. Here are a few examples of how this principle is expressed in the Bible:

1. **Proverbs 26:27**: "The trap you set for others will be the trap you get caught in yourself. If you roll a boulder down on anyone, it will roll back and crush you." This verse illustrates the idea that harm done to others, whether through hateful words or actions, can ultimately result in harm coming back to the person who initiated it.
2. **Galatians 6:7**: "Do not be deceived: God cannot be mocked. And man reaps what he sows." This verse emphasizes the principle of sowing and reaping, indicating that the consequences of our actions, including the use of hateful words and deeds, will come back to us in some form.
3. **Luke 6:38**: "Give, and it will be given to you. With good measure, it's pressed down, it's shaken together, and it's running over, and will be poured into your lap. For with the measure you use, the same will be measured to you." This verse magnifies the idea that our actions towards others, whether positive or negative, will be returned to us in a similar manner.

Overall, the Bible teaches that hateful words and actions can have consequences not only for others but also for the person who engages in them. It is important to be mindful of our words and behavior, treating others with love, kindness, and respect, in order to avoid the negative consequences that can result from sowing seeds of hatred and harm.

CHAPTER 13

"Deceitful ways will be discovered, and justice will prevail."

Discovering deceitful ways and ensuring that justice prevails can be achieved through a combination of vigilance, investigation, evidence gathering, and legal action. It is important not to be deceitful for several reasons:

1. **Ethical reasons**: Deceitful behavior goes against moral and ethical principles. Being deceitful involves dishonesty, manipulation, and betrayal, which can harm others and damage trust and relationships.
2. **Legal consequences**: Deceitful actions can lead to legal repercussions, including criminal charges, civil lawsuits, and financial penalties. Perpetrators of deceitful behavior may face criminal prosecution and imprisonment.
3. **Personal integrity**: Acting with honesty and integrity is essential for personal growth and development. Deceitful behavior can damage one's reputation, self-esteem, and relationships. Being truthful and transparent builds character and fosters trust and respect.
4. **Protection of rights**: Justice ensures that the rights and interests of individuals are protected and upheld. By holding deceitful individuals accountable for their actions, justice helps to prevent further harm and ensure that victims receive restitution and redress.

In conclusion, it is crucial to refrain from deceitful behavior, adhere to ethical principles, and uphold justice to promote a just and fair society where individuals are held accountable for their actions. Justice must prevail to protect the rights and well-being of all members of society.

Furthermore, the Bible teaches that deceitfulness is sinful and unjust, as it involves deception, manipulation, and betrayal. It is important to be truthful, honest, and act with integrity in all aspects of life to prevent injustice and uphold God's commandments.

CHAPTER 14

"Do not be hesitant to teach the one desiring to hear your testimony."

1. **Sharing your testimony can inspire, guide, and encourage others**: by sharing your story, you may help others see that they are not alone in their struggles and that there is hope for them as well. Your testimony may contain valuable lessons or insights that can help the person navigate their own challenges or struggles.
2. **It can strengthen your own faith**: Sharing your testimony can help you reflect on the work that God has done in your life and remind you of His faithfulness. In turn you may gain further insight that you can apply to your walk with God.
3. **It can lead others to faith**: Your testimony may be the key that opens the door for someone else to start their journey with God. Hearing about your faith and journey and experiences with God may inspire the person to deepen their own relationship with Him and help them grow in their faith.
4. **It is a way to fulfill the Great Commission**: Jesus commands us to go and make disciples of all nations, and sharing your testimony is a powerful way to do this.
5. **It can cultivate a sense of community**: Sharing a testimony can foster a sense of belonging and unity among believers, as it creates an opportunity for others to share their stories, promoting growth and support for one another.

6. **It can offer encouragement and hope**: hearing about how God has worked in your life can give the person hope that God can also work in their own life in a similar way. You will have the opportunity to teach them how to overcome obstacles and hardships that they may endure.

7. **It can foster a sense of connection**: sharing a testimony can create a bond between you and the person, as they may feel understood or supported in their own journey. This will open the door for them to be more receptive to hearing and learning from your experiences.

8. **It can bring about transformation**: your testimony has the potential to impact the person in a positive way, leading them to make positive changes in their own life and to draw closer to God.

CHAPTER 15

"Extend mercy and forgiveness to the one who has wronged you."

Extending mercy and forgiveness to someone who has wronged you is important for several reasons:

1. **Healing and inner peace**: holding on to anger and resentment can be harmful to your mental and emotional well-being. By extending mercy and forgiveness, you will release the negative emotions and allow yourself to heal and find inner peace.
2. **Building relationships**: forgiveness can help repair and strengthen relationships. It shows that you are willing to move past the hurt and work towards rebuilding trust and understanding with the person who wronged you.
3. **Promoting empathy and understanding**: This can foster a deeper understanding of their actions and motivations, leading to greater compassion and connection.
4. **Breaking the cycle of harm**: By choosing to forgive, you can break the cycle of retaliation and harm. Responding to wrongdoing with forgiveness can inspire positive change and promote peace within yourself and in your relationships.
5. **Personal growth**: Extending mercy and forgiveness requires strength and courage. It can be a transformative experience that allows you to grow and learn from the situation, ultimately making you a stronger and more compassionate individual.

Overall, extending mercy and forgiveness to someone who has wronged you can lead to healing, reconciliation, personal growth, and the promotion of positive and peaceful relationships. It can also help break the cycle of harm and lead to a greater sense of empathy and understanding.

CHAPTER 16

"Use kindness and truth to find favor amongst those who are in leadership positions."

Using kindness and truth with those in leadership positions is necessary for a few key reasons:

1. **Establishing trust**: Kindness and truthfulness help to build trust with those in leadership positions. When leaders see that you are genuine and honest in your interactions, they are more likely to trust you and your intentions.
2. **Building positive relationships**: Being kind and truthful creates a positive relationship with leaders. This can lead to more open communication, collaboration, and ultimately, a better working relationship.
3. **Demonstrating integrity**: Kindness and truthfulness demonstrate your integrity and character to leaders. By consistently displaying these qualities, you show that you can be trusted to act in an ethical and responsible manner.
4. **Influencing others**: Leaders are more likely to favor those who exhibit kindness and truth because these qualities can have a positive influence on those around them. By being positive and truthful, you can help create a positive and productive environment.

Overall, using kindness and truth to find favor among those in leadership positions is essential for building trust, establishing positive relationships, demonstrating integrity, and influencing others in a positive way.

CHAPTER 17

SELF

"Do not lack the proper rest needed to eliminate confusion and uneasiness."

When you lack the proper rest needed it can negatively impact your cognitive function, your memory, and your concentration. This can also lead to confusion, difficulty making decisions, and trouble processing information.

In addition, inadequate sleep can also affect your mood and your emotional well-being, leading to feelings of irritability, anxiety, depression, and uneasiness. When your overall brain function is impaired because of the lack of proper rest you cannot perform your general mission at your full capacity.

CHAPTER 18

"Cleanse your body with an herbal detox."

Cleansing your body with an herbal detox has proven to have several benefits.

1. **Cleanse your body with an herbal detox to eliminate toxins**. Herbal detoxes can help your body eliminate toxins that accumulate from environmental pollutants, processed foods and other sources. By purging these toxins through detoxification, the body and mind may function more efficiently and effectively.
2. **Cleanse your body with the herbal detox to improve digestion**. Herbal detoxes often include ingredients that support digestive health, such as fiber and digestive enzymes. This can help to promote better digestion and absorption of nutrients from food.
3. **Cleanse your body with the herbal detox to boost your energy levels**. An herbal detox can increase energy levels by helping your body rid itself of waste and toxins that may be weighing it down or causing fatigue.
4. **Cleanse your body with an herbal detox to support weight loss**. Herbal detoxes are sometimes used as a way to jump start a weight loss program or to cleanse the body after a period of indulgence. By eliminating excess waste and toxins, the body may be better able to metabolize and burn fat more efficiently.

Here are the most common ways to detox your body using herbal remedies.

1. **Herbal teas**: Drinking herbal teas made from detoxifying herbs such as dandelion, ginger, turmeric, or milk Thistle can help support the body's natural detoxification processes. These teas can help to cleanse the liver, kidneys, and digestive system.
2. **Herbal supplements**: There are many herbal supplements available that support detoxification, such as spirulina, chlorella, and activated charcoal. These supplements can help to bind to toxins and help the body eliminate them more effectively.
3. **Detox baths**: Adding herbs such as Epsom salt, ginger, or lavender to a bath can help to detoxify the body through the skin. These herbs will also help to relax the body and promote sweating, which can eliminate toxins.
4. **Herbal tinctures**: Herbal tinctures are concentrated liquid extracts of herbs that are taken orally. You can find detoxifying tinctures that contain herbs like burdock root, cleavers, or echinacea, which can help support the detoxification process.
5. **Herbal cleanses**: There are many herbal cleanse kits available that contain a combination of herbs, fiber, and other ingredients designed to support detoxification. These cleanses usually last for a specific period of time and are meant to give the digestive system a break, by supporting the elimination of toxins.

It is important to note that while herbal remedies can be a natural way to support detoxification, it is still important to maintain a healthy diet, stay hydrated, exercise regularly and practice other healthy habits in order to support overall health and wellness. It is always best to consult with the health care professional before starting any detox program, especially if you have any underlying health conditions.

Some people detox once a week, others may detox once a month, and some just a few times a year. How often you detox is at your discretion. If you are frequently experiencing symptoms of toxicity, such as fatigue, moodiness, mental fog, and abdominal bloating, more frequent detoxing is a smart choice. Always drink 8 to 10 glasses of water a day to stay hydrated and aid in a healthy wellbeing.

Detoxification can also improve your mental health. It can help those that suffer from PTSD, depression, and many addictions. Detoxification is a cleansing or purification process. Toxins can impair physical organ function and have a negative effect on your mental well-being and cognitive function. Experiencing trauma is toxic, such as in toxic relationships. This can cause stress, and stress will create inflammation and metabolic byproducts that will not be as easy to discharge or eliminate from the body.

During trauma some people are exposed to chemical and biological toxins during the course of the traumatic experience such as in war, natural disasters, abuse, and in genocide. Using toxic substances such as alcohol, and drugs can also have a negative effect on one's physical and mental health and including their brain function.

Poor quality nutrition and eating without a healthy diet can also contribute to the buildup of toxins in your body. The liver and skin are major organs of detoxification in the body. They are the largest human organs and the primary organs of detoxification. The skin protects you against microorganisms, ultraviolet light, dehydration, and mechanical damage. The skin is a physical barrier for the human body against the external environment.

The liver makes fat soluble toxins water soluble by activating the cytochrome P-450 enzymes. These enzymes are attached to toxins and prepare them for the next phase of detoxification where they are then excreted by the kidneys. Burdock. Purslane, Dandelion, and Bitterroot are good herbs for using to detox the liver. Vegetables that you can eat that are helpful in supporting the elimination of toxins are cabbage, broccoli, brussels sprouts, onions, and garlic, both raw and cooked. Onions and garlic should be used daily.

Stay away from bread and yeast-based products because they can cause toxicity, especially for those sensitive to alcohol. The yeast ferments sugar into alcohol and endogenous alcohol production is high after eating foods rich in carbohydrates. Yeast converts the alcohol into acetaldehyde affecting levels of gut flora and leading to chronic Candidiasis. To all my bread lovers, I am sorry to disappoint you but the yeast in the bread is toxic to your body!

Seaweed is one of the most important detoxification foods because they

34

bind toxins in the intestinal tract. You can add seaweed to many meal recipes or eat it in plain form.

CHAPTER 19

"Beware of the smooth talker. Your destruction is the ultimate attempt."

The destruction caused by smooth talkers is often considered insidious and harmful because their charismatic and persuasive nature allows them to manipulate and deceive others with ease. They are able to easily gain trust and manipulate situations to their advantage, making the consequences of their actions influential and damaging. The charm and charisma of a smooth talker can create a false sense of security and make it difficult for others to see through their manipulative tactics until it is too late. The destruction caused by the smooth talker is considered more destructive because it is often unexpected and goes unnoticed until the damage is already done.

Recognizing the smooth talker can be challenging, as they are skilled at manipulating and deceiving others with their charm and persuasive abilities. However, there are some common signs to look out for:

1. **Charismatic and charming**: Smooth talkers tend to be extremely charismatic and charming, able to easily win over others with their personality.
2. **Quick wit and eloquent speech**: They are often quick thinkers and have a way with words and are able to talk their way out of any situation or make convincing arguments.
3. **Flattery and compliments**: Smooth talkers often use flattery and compliments to manipulate others and gain their trust.
4. **Unwillingness to take responsibility**: They may try to shift blame or

avoid taking responsibility for their actions, using their charm to deflect criticism.

5. **Inconsistent behavior**: A smooth talker may say one thing but do another, leading to inconsistencies in their behavior and actions.

6. **Overuse of excuses**: They may frequently make excuses for their behavior or actions, using their charm to justify their actions.

7. **Lack of empathy**: Smooth talkers may lack genuine empathy for others, using their charm to manipulate people for their own gain.

By being mindful of these signs and trusting your instincts, you may be able to recognize a smooth talker before they are able to manipulate or deceive you.

CHAPTER 20

Pay off your debts. Do not be a borrower."

Paying off your debts and avoiding borrowing can have several benefits which include:

1. **Financial freedom**: By paying off your debts, you can free yourself from the burden of owing money to others. This will provide a sense of financial security and independence.
2. **Avoiding high interest payments**: Borrowing money often comes with high interest rates, which can add up over time and cost you more money in the long run. By paying off your debts and avoiding borrowing, you can save money on interest payments.
3. **Improving credit score**: Paying off your debt can have a positive impact on your credit score, making it easier to qualify for loans or credit in the future. A good credit score can also help you secure better interest rates on loans and credit cards.
4. **Reduce stress**: Debt can be a significant source of stress and anxiety for many people. By paying off your debts and avoiding borrowing, you can reduce financial stress and improve your overall well-being.
5. **Building wealth**: By avoiding borrowing and paying off your debts, you can free up more money to save and invest. Building wealth through saving and investing can provide long term financial security and help you achieve your financial goals.

Paying off your debt and avoiding borrowing can lead to greater financial stability, reduce stress, and a stronger financial future. It is important to manage your finances responsibly and make sound decisions to ensure your long-term financial well-being.

CHAPTER 21

"End procrastination and work diligently towards your goals."

Ending procrastination and working diligently towards your goals can have several benefits including:

1. **Increase productivity**: When you stop procrastinating and start working diligently towards your goals, you are able to accomplish more a less time. This can help you make progress towards your goals at a faster pace and be more efficient in your work.
2. **Improved time management**: By eliminating procrastination and working diligently, you can better prioritize your tasks and manage your time effectively. This can help you focus on what needs to be done and avoid wasting time on unimportant or non-urgent tasks.
3. **Enhanced motivation and focus**: Working diligently towards your goals can help you stay focused and motivated to achieve them. As you make progress and see results, you are likely to feel more inspired and committed to continuing your efforts.
4. **Reduced stress and anxiety**: Procrastination can lead to increased stress and anxiety as deadlines approach and tasks pile up. By working diligently towards your goals, you can reduce the pressure and overwhelmed feelings that often comes with procrastination.

5. **Achieving success**: When you are consistent and committed to working diligently towards your goals, you are more likely to achieve success and reach your desired outcomes. Diligence, perseverance, and hard work are key ingredients for achieving success in any endeavor.

It is important to set clear goals, create a plan of action, and stay committed to making progress every day towards achieving your goals.

CHAPTER 22

"Do not be restless and noisy with loud talking. This is irritating to others."

Having noisy and restless behavior, including loud talking, can be irritating to other people for several reasons:

1. **Disruption of peace and quiet**: Constant loud talking and restlessness can disrupt the peace and quiet of a shared space, such as an office or home, making it difficult for others to focus or relax.
2. **Lack of consideration for others**: Noisy behavior may be seen as inconsiderate of others needs and preferences. Loud talking and restlessness can be seen as selfish actions that prioritize your wants over the comfort and well-being of those around you.
3. **Distraction and annoyance**: Loud talking and restlessness can be distracting and annoying to others, particularly if they are trying to concentrate, have a conversation, or engage in a quiet activity.
4. **Disruption of social dynamics**: Loud behavior may disrupt social interactions and dynamics, making it challenging for others to have meaningful conversations or connect with each other in a harmonious way.
5. **Impact on productivity and efficiency**: Noisy and restless behavior can impact productivity and efficiency, as it may make it difficult for others to focus on their work or tasks without being distracted by the constant noise and movement.

Noisy and restless behavior, particularly loud talking, can be irritating to other people by disrupting peace and quiet, showing a lack of consideration for others, causing distraction and annoyance, disrupting social dynamics, and impacting productivity and efficiency. It is important for you to be mindful of your behavior and considerate of the needs and preferences of those around you to maintain positive relationships and a harmonious environment.

CHAPTER 23

"Find true happiness by rejoicing in your own accomplishments."

Finding true happiness by rejoicing in your own accomplishments involves recognizing and celebrating your successes, big or small, and finding contentment and fulfillment within yourself. Here are some ways to achieve this:

1. **Practice self-compassion:** Be kind and compassionate towards yourself, acknowledging your efforts and progress rather than constantly focusing on your shortcomings or comparing yourself to others.
2. **Set realistic goals:** Set achievable goals that are meaningful to you and work towards them step by step. Celebrate the small victories along the way and acknowledge your progress.
3. **Cultivate gratitude:** Focus on what you have accomplished and express gratitude for your abilities, opportunities, and achievements. Gratitude can help shift your perspective towards a positive outlook on life.
4. **Build self-confidence:** Recognize your strengths and abilities, and trust in your capabilities to overcome challenges and achieve your goals. Confidence in yourself can boost your happiness and satisfaction with your accomplishments.
5. **Practice self-reflection:** Take time to reflect on your achievements and how they have positively impacted your life. Acknowledge the hard work and dedication that went into reaching your goals.
6. **Surrounding yourself with positivity:** Surround yourself with support-

ive and encouraging people who celebrate your accomplishments and uplift you. Their positivity can reinforce your sense of happiness and fulfillment.

7. **Focus on personal growth:** Do not put emphasis on the validation of others, instead, focus on your personal growth and development. Set goals that align with your values and aspirations, and work towards becoming the best version of yourself.

8. **Embrace imperfection:** Accept that perfection is unattainable, and that mistakes and setbacks are a natural part of the journey towards success. Embrace imperfection as an opportunity for growth and learning.

By rejoicing in your own accomplishments and finding happiness within yourself, you can cultivate a sense of fulfilment, purpose, and contentment that is not solely dependent on external validation or the opinions of others. Celebrate your successes, practice self-love and gratitude, and continue to strive towards personal growth and self-improvement to enhance your happiness and well-being.

CHAPTER 24

"Hold on to your integrity and moral character, even if it is against the grain."

Holding on to your integrity and moral character, even when it goes against the grain, it's important for several reasons:

1. **Personal satisfaction:** Acting in alignment with your values and principles brings a sense of personal satisfaction and self-respect. Knowing that you have stayed true to yourself, and your beliefs can boost your self-esteem and overall well-being.
2. **Building trust and credibility:** Consistently demonstrating integrity and moral character earns the trust and respect of others. People are more likely to trust and follow someone who is honest, reliable, and ethical in their actions, even if it means going against popular opinion.
3. **Setting a positive example:** By staying true to your values and moral compass, you set a positive example for others to follow. Your integrity can inspire and influence those around you to prioritize ethical behavior and uphold their own moral standards.
4. **Avoiding regret and guilt:** Acting with integrity and moral character helps you avoid feelings of regret, guilt, or shame that may arise from compromising your values for the sake of conformity or approval. Living authentically and ethically can lead to a clear conscience and peace of mind.

5. **Building resilience and inner strength:** Upholding your integrity in the face of adversity or opposition can build resilience and inner strength. It requires courage and conviction to stick to your principles when they are challenged, but doing so can strengthen your character and steadfastness.

6. **Long term success and fulfillment:** Maintaining integrity and moral character sets the foundation for long term success and fulfillment. People who consistently act ethically and with integrity are more likely to achieve lasting success, build meaningful relationships and experience genuine happiness.

Holding on to your integrity and moral character, even when it goes against the grain, is a reflection of your true self and what you stand for. It defines your character and shapes your interactions with others, contributing to life of authenticity, respect, and fulfillment.

CHAPTER 25

"Welcome into your being the spirit of calmness."

Welcoming the spirit of calmness into your being involves cultivating practices and habits that promote inner peace and tranquility. Here are some suggestions to help you invite calmness into your life:

1. **Mindfulness and meditation:** Practicing mindfulness and meditation can help you stay present in the moment and cultivate a sense of inner calm. Set aside time each day to meditate or practice mindfulness techniques such as deep breathing, body scans, or focused awareness.
2. **Physical exercise:** Engaging in regular physical exercise such as yoga, walking, or jogging, can help release built up tension and promote a sense of relaxation. Exercise will also boost your mood and reduce stress levels.
3. **Breathe work:** Deep breathing exercises can help calm the mind and body by activating the body's relaxation response. Practice deep breathing techniques such as diaphragmatic breathing, alternate nostril breathing, or box breathing to promote calmness and reduce anxiety.
4. **Gratitude practice:** Cultivating a sense of gratitude can shift your focus towards positive aspects of your life and promote feelings of peace and contentment. Take time each day to reflect on things you are grateful for and express gratitude towards yourself and others.
5. **Connect with nature:** Spending time in nature can have a calming effect

on the mind and body. Take a walk in the park, sit by a lake, or simply observe the beauty of the natural world to soothe your spirit and promote relaxation.

6. **Set boundaries:** Establishing healthy boundaries and prioritizing self-care can help protect your peace of mind and prevent becoming overwhelmed. Learn to say no to commitments that do not align with your values or priorities and make time for activities that nourish your soul.

7. **Practice self-compassion:** Treat yourself with kindness and compassion, especially during times of stress or difficulty. Practice self-care rituals that nurture your well-being, such as taking a warm bath, journaling, or engaging in a hobby you will enjoy.

8. **Seek support:** Don't hesitate to reach out for help if you are feeling overwhelmed or struggling to find calmness in your life. Talk to a trusted friend, counselor, or therapist for support and guidance in navigating challenging emotions.

By incorporating these practices into your daily routine and mindset, you can create a welcoming space for the spirit of calmness to enter your being and cultivate a greater sense of peace and serenity in your life.

CHAPTER 26

"Do good so good will return to you. If you sow bad seed, bad will return to you."

The energy you put out, whether positive or negative, is the energy you will have returned to you. This is referred to as the law of karma or the concept of cause and effect.

In the Bible, the concept of sowing and reaping is a common theme that is often used to illustrate the principle of cause and effect. It is stating that the actions we take, whether positive or negative, will have consequences in our lives.

Galatians 6:7-8, says, "Do not be misled: It is impossible to ignore God and get away with it. You will definitely reap what you sow. Everyone who lives to only satisfy their own fleshy and sinful desires, will reap destruction; but those who live to please God through spirit and truth, will reap everlasting life from the Spirit of God."

This passage emphasizes the importance of our intentions and actions, as they will ultimately determine the outcomes we experience.

From a biblical perspective, sowing bad seed refers to engaging in sinful or immoral behavior that goes against God's will. This can lead to negative consequences, such as hardship, suffering and separation from God. On the other hand, sowing good seed involves living a righteous and obedient life in accordance with God's commandments. This can lead to blessings, fulfillment, and a closer relationship with God.

The principle of sowing and reaping is not just about immediate rewards or punishments, but also about the long-term consequences of our actions. While God is loving and merciful, he also holds us accountable for our choices and actions. By sowing good seed through acts of kindness, generosity, and righteousness, we can experience the grace and blessings of God in our lives. It is a reminder to strive for goodness and righteousness in all that we do, knowing that God sees our hearts and will reward us accordingly.

Here is how this concept works:

1. **Intention and action:** When you act with kindness, compassion, and integrity, you are sending out positive energy into the world. This positive energy can have a ripple effect, leading to more positive interactions and experiences in your life. On the other hand, if you act with malice, dishonesty, or selfishness, you are likely to attract negative energy and experiences.

2. **Law of attraction:** The law of attraction states that what you put out is what you get back, meaning that the energy you emit - whether positive or negative - will return to you in some form. If you are able to maintain a positive mindset and focus on goodness and positivity, you are more likely to attract favorable outcomes and experiences into your life.

3. **Growth and learning:** The concept of karma also emphasizes personal growth and learning from your actions and experiences. By being mindful of your intentions and the impact of your actions on others, you can cultivate self-awareness, empathy, and compassion. This awareness can lead to greater harmony in your relationships and a deeper sense of fulfillment and well-being.

Always act with integrity, kindness, and compassion in all aspects of your life. By aligning your actions with positive values and intentions, you can create a more harmonious and fulfilling existence for yourself and those around you.

CHAPTER 27

"Drop the pride. Drop the ego. Humble yourself."

To drop pride, ego, and humble yourself, it is important to cultivate a mindset of humility and modesty. Here are some steps that you can take to achieve this:

1. **Self-reflection:** Take the time to reflect on your thoughts, actions, and behaviors. Be honest with yourself about areas where pride and ego may be influencing your decisions.
2. **Practice gratitude:** Acknowledge and appreciate the blessings and opportunities in your life. Cultivating a sense of gratitude can help shift your focus away from yourself and towards others.
3. **Serve others:** Engage in acts of service and kindness towards others. Volunteering, helping those in need, and showing compassion are great ways to practice humility.
4. **Listen and learn:** Be open to feedback and perspectives from others. Listen actively and seek to understand different viewpoints, even if they challenge your own beliefs.
5. **Let go of perfectionism:** Accept that you are not perfect and that it is OK to make mistakes. Embrace humility by being willing to learn and grow from your experiences.
6. **Practice forgiveness:** Let go of grudges and resentments towards others. Forgiveness can help you release negative feelings and promote peace

within yourself.

7. **Practice mindfulness:** Pay attention to your thoughts and emotions and learn to detach yourself from ego driven desires and insecurities. Mindfulness can help you stay present and connected to the world around you.

8. **Seek spiritual guidance:** Pray, meditate, or engage in spiritual practices that help you connect with a higher power and cultivate a sense of humility and surrender.

By practicing these steps consistently and intentionally, you can gradually let go of pride ego, and cultivate a spirit of humility and openness towards others. Remember that humility is a lifelong journey, and it requires effort and self-awareness to maintain a humble mindset in all aspects of your life.

CHAPTER 28

"Receive instruction and discipline. It will make you a better person."

Receiving instruction and discipline can make you a better person in several ways:

1. **Personal growth:** Instruction and discipline can provide you with valuable guidance and feedback on areas where you can improve. By being open to instruction and disciplined, you can learn from your mistakes and shortcomings, and grow personally and professionally.
2. **Accountability:** Receiving instruction and discipline holds you accountable for your actions and behaviors. It helps you take responsibility for your decisions and motivates you to make positive changes in your life.
3. **Humility:** Being willing to receive instruction and discipline requires humility and a willingness to learn from others. It can help you develop a sense of humility and openness towards feedback and criticism.
4. **Character development:** Instruction and discipline can shape your character and help you develop important qualities such as resilience, perseverance, and self-discipline. By embracing feedback and guidance, you can become a stronger and more well-rounded individual.
5. **Building relationships:** Receiving instruction and discipline can improve your relationships with others. It shows that you are open to feedback and willing to make changes based on others input, which can strengthen your connections with friends, family, and colleagues.

6. **Achieving goals:** Instruction and discipline can help you stay focused and motivated towards achieving your goals. By following guidance and taking feedback seriously, you can make progress towards your goals more effectively and efficiently.

Being open to receiving instruction and discipline can help you become a better person by promoting personal growth, accountability, humility, character development, relationship building, and goal achievement. It is important to approach feedback and guidance with an open mind and a willingness to learn and grow from the experience.

Proverbs 10:17

"Whoever heeds instruction is on the path to life, but he who rejects reproof leads others astray".

Proverbs 19:20–21

"Listen to advice and accept discipline, and at the end you will be counted among the wise".

Proverbs 16:20

"Those who listen to instruction will prosper."

CHAPTER 29

"When you fall, be not dismayed, just get up. Like a baby learning to walk, it is the necessary process to grow."

The phrase "when you fall be not dismayed just get up" lets us know that setbacks and failures are a natural part of the learning and growth process.

Just like a baby learning to walk, stumbling and falling down are essential steps in the journey towards mastering a new skill. Instead of feeling discouraged or defeated by setbacks, it is important to pick yourself up, dust yourself off, and keep moving forward.

Learning to walk requires persistence, resilience, and a willingness to try again despite previous failures. Babies do not give up after falling down multiple times; Instead, they keep trying until they eventually succeed. In the same way, when faced with challenges or obstacles in life, it is important to adopt a similar mindset of perseverance and determination.

By embracing failure as a necessary part of the growth process, individuals can develop important skills such as resilience, determination, and perseverance. Each setback offers an opportunity to learn, grow, and improve. Just as a baby learns to walk by getting up after each fall, individuals can overcome challenges and setbacks by staying resilient, learning from their mistakes, and continuing to move forward towards their goals.

This phrase encourages individuals to see setbacks and failures as opportunities for growth and learning. Rather than being discouraged by failure, individuals should embrace it as a natural part of the journey towards success and personal development. Just like a baby learning to walk, the process of getting up after a fall is a necessary step towards growth and self-improvement.

CHAPTER 30

"Use self-control. Do not be quick tempered and act foolishly."

If you don't use self-control and act foolishly and quick-tempered, you may end up making poor decisions that can have negative consequences on yourself and others. You may say or do things that you later regret, damage relationships, harm others, and create unnecessary conflicts.

There is a chance you can face legal consequences, damage your reputation, and suffer from the fallout of your actions. Ultimately, lack of self-control and acting recklessly can lead to a host of problems and setbacks in your personal and professional life. It is important to practice self-control and think before acting in order to avoid these negative outcomes.

In other words, self-control is necessary because it acts as a shield of protection for you.

When you have the ability to exercise restraint and think before you act, you have mastered a temperament that is very hard for most to learn and control. The benefits of this are immeasurable.

CHAPTER 31

"Do not be naïve and believe everything that you hear. Do not be easily misled."

Being naïve and easily misled can lead to undesirable consequences. Here are some reasons why you should not believe everything you hear and be cautious before trusting information:

1. **People might have ulterior motives**: Some individuals may spread false information or manipulate the truth to serve their own interests. By blindly believing everything you hear, you might fall victim to deceitful tactics.
2. **Misinformation and fake news**: In today's digital age, misinformation and fake news are rampant. It is essential to fact-check and verify information before accepting it as the truth.
3. **Bias and prejudice**: People's perspectives and beliefs can shape the information they share. It is crucial to consider different viewpoints and sources to gain a comprehensive understanding of a topic.
4. **Lack of credibility**: Not all sources of information are reliable and trustworthy. It is important to verify the credibility of the source before accepting the information as accurate.
5. **Personal growth and critical thinking**: Being critical and questioning the information you receive can help develop your critical thinking skills. It is

essential to analyze information critically and make informed decisions based on facts and evidence.

Always verify facts before believing everything you hear. Pay attention to the actions of others and be sure their actions are in line with what they say.

Being cautious and discerning can help protect you from being misled and make better-informed decisions.

Proverbs 14:15-22

Only the Simpleton's believe every word they hear! The wise think about what they do before they do it. A wise man suspects danger and cautiously avoids evil. Wise people are careful and stay out of trouble, but fools are careless and quick to act, foolishly plunging ahead and with confidence. Those who have short tempers do foolish things but someone with understanding remains calm. Schemers who plot and have wicked plans are hated. If you are a fool, you will be rewarded with foolishness, but the wise are rewarded with knowledge. Evil people will bow down to those who are good; the wicked will bow down at the door of those who do right. The poor are despised even by their neighbors, while the rich have many friends. It is a sin to hate your neighbor; but being kind to the needy brings happiness. Those who make evil plans will be ruined, but those who plan to do good will be loved and trusted.

Pay attention to the red flags. Don't dismiss your intuition.

CHAPTER 32

"A person with a calm and peaceful spirit brings life and health to their body. Evilness, jealousy, and envy are life rottenness that seeps into the marrow of the bones."

A calm and peaceful spirit has been shown to have numerous positive effects on both mental and physical health. When a person is in a state of tranquility and contentment, their body can relax, releasing stress and tension that can contribute to various health issues such as high blood pressure, heart disease, and weakened immune system. Additionally, a peaceful spirit can improve quality of sleep, digestion, and overall well-being.

On the other hand, evilness, jealousy, and envy are negative emotions that can have destructive effects on the body. These emotions can create chronic stress, which can weaken the immune system, disrupt hormonal balance, and increase the risk of various diseases. Furthermore, dwelling on negative emotions can lead to bitterness and resentment, which can affect relationships and overall mental health.

As the saying goes, "a merry heart doeth good like a medicine, but a broken spirit drieth the bones." Having a peaceful spirit can bring life and health to the body, while evilness, jealousy, and envy can lead to rottenness that seeps into the marrow of the bones, causing physical and emotional harm. It is essential to cultivate positive emotions and maintain a peaceful spirit in order to promote health and well-being.

CHAPTER 33

"Remember that you are always being watched."

In this day and time, we are constantly being watched in various ways due to advancements in technology and the widespread use of surveillance systems. Here are some common ways in which we are being monitored:

1. **Security cameras**: Security cameras are prevalent in public spaces, businesses, and even residential areas. They are used for surveillance

purposes and can capture our movements and activities.

2. **Social media**: Many people share details of their lives on social media platforms, which can be accessed by a wide audience. Companies and individuals can track our online activities, interests, and interactions.

3. **Smartphone and devices:** Our smartphones and other devices often have built-in features that track our locations, search history, and online behavior. This data can be used to target advertisements or analyze our habits.

4. **Internet browsing**: Websites and online services often collect data about our browsing habits and online activities through cookies and tracking technologies. This information can be used for targeted advertising and analytics.

5. **Smart home devices**: Smart home devices such as voice assistance and connected appliances can also collect data about our daily routines and activities. This data can be used to improve user experience but also raises privacy concerns.

6. **Public Wi-Fi networks**: When we connect to public Wi-Fi networks our Internet traffic can be monitored and tracked by third parties. This can potentially lead to data breaches and cyber security risk.

7. **Workplace monitoring**: Employers may monitor employee's activities, communication, and Internet usage while on the job. This is done to ensure productivity, security, and compliance with company policies.

It is very important to be mindful of the ways in which we are being watched and modest society and take steps to protect our privacy and personal information. Understanding the potential risk and being cautious about sharing sensitive data can help safeguard our digital footprint and maintain a sense of control over our privacy.

Our actions also have an impact on others; therefore, we should strive to be positive role models. The motivation for living a good lifestyle should come from within and be driven through being a person of integrity, building strong and good relationships with others, contributing positively to society, setting a positive example for others, and by being very mindful of how our actions are perceived by others.

Always be willing to focus on your own self-improvement and align your actions with your values. By doing so you can lead a fulfilling and personal life that positively impacts both yourself and those around you.

Psalms 121:8 says, "the Lord keeps watch over you as you come and go, both now and forever."

Psalms 33:13-15 says, "From heaven the Lord looks down and sees all mankind from his dwelling place he watches all who live on earth - he who forms the hearts of all, who considers everything they do."

"Meditate on good things in a quiet place often. It rejuvenates the mind."

Meditating on good things in a quiet place can have a rejuvenating effect on your mind for several reasons:

1. **Stress Reduction**: Taking time to focus on positive thoughts and gratitude can help reduce stress and anxiety. By shifting your attention away from negative or worrisome thoughts and focusing on positive aspects of your life, you can create a sense of calm and relaxation.

2. **Mindfulness and presence**: Meditation involves being fully present in the moment and cultivating awareness of your thoughts and emotions. By meditating on good things in a quiet place, you can train your mind to be more present and focused, leading to a greater sense of clarity and mental rejuvenation.

3. **Positive thinking**: Focusing on positive thoughts and feelings during meditation can help shift your mindset towards a more optimistic and thoughtful outlook. This can improve your mood, increase feelings of satisfaction and contentment, and foster a more positive mindset in your daily life.

4. **Emotional regulation**: Meditation can help you develop emotional regulation skills, allowing you to better manage your emotions and respond to challenges with greater resilience and calmness. By meditating on good things, you can cultivate positive emotions and strengthen your ability to navigate difficult situations with a more balanced perspective.

5. **Brain health**: Research has shown that meditation practices can have positive effects on brain health, including increased brain connectivity, improved cognitive function, and reduced age-related cognitive decline. Meditating on good things and the quiet place can help promote mental clarity, focus, and overall brain health.

6. **Self-care and well-being**: Taking time for self-care, such as meditating on positive thoughts, is an essential aspect of maintaining overall well-being. By prioritizing moments of quiet reflection and mindfulness, you can nourish your mental and emotional health, recharge your energy, and cultivate a sense of inner peace hand balance.

Regularly meditating on good things in a quiet place can rejuvenate your mind by reducing stress, promoting mindfulness, fostering positive thinking, enhancing emotional regulation, improving brain health, and supporting overall well-being. By incorporating meditation into your daily routine, you can create a space for mental rejuvenation, self-care, and inner peace.

CHAPTER 34

"Be of good cheer and smile. It warms the heart of the onlooker."

Being of good cheer and smiling can warm the heart of the onlooker in several ways:

1. **Positive energy**: When you exude good cheer and positivity through your actions and smile, you emit a contagious energy that can uplift the mood of those around you. Your warmth and enthusiasm can create a welcoming and inviting atmosphere, making others feel comfortable and valued.
2. **Connection**: Smiling and being cheerful can create a sense of connection and report with the onlooker. A genuine smile and friendly demeanor can convey openness, friendliness, and approachability, fostering a sense of warmth and connection between you and the other person.
3. **Emotional contagion**: Emotions are contagious, and when you display happiness and positivity through your smile and cheerful attitude, others are likely to mirror those emotions. Your smile can't evoke a positive emotional response in the onlooker, leading to a ripple effect of happiness and warmth.
4. **Stress reduction**: Smiling and being cheerful can help alleviate stress

and tension for both you and the onlooker. A warm smile and positive attitude can signal to the other person that everything is OK and create a sense of ease and relaxation, promoting a more positive and common environment.

5. **Positive reinforcement**: Your good cheer and smile can serve as positive reinforcement for the onlooker's behavior or mood. When you respond with kindness, enthusiasm, and a smile, you validate the other person's presence and contribute to their sense of well-being and self-worth.

6. **Enhanced communication**: Smiling and being cheerful can enhance communication and facilitate positive interactions. Your smile can signal openness, friendliness, and receptivity, making it easier for the onlooker to engage with you and feel comfortable expressing themselves.

7. **Mood improvement**: Smiling and being in good cheer have been shown to stimulate the release of endorphins, the body's feel-good hormones. By sharing your positive energy and warm smile, you can help brighten the onlooker's mood and promote a sense of happiness and well-being.

Being a good cheerful person and smiling can warm the heart of the onlooker by emitting positive energy, fostering connection, evoking positive emotions, reducing stress, providing positive reinforcement, enhancing communication, and boosting mood. Your cheerful demeanor and warm smile could have a ripple effect on those around you, spreading joy, positivity, and a sense of connection and goodwill.

CHAPTER 35

"Pray, pray, and always pray!"

Prank can have numerous positive benefits for individuals. Here are some reasons why it is very beneficial to make prayer a regular practice:

1. **Connection with God**: Prayer is considered a way to communicate with God, or a Higher Power. This connection can provide comfort, guidance, and a sense of purpose in life.
2. **Reflection and gratitude**: Praying can help individuals pause and reflect on their lives, expressing gratitude for blessings received and acknowledging challenges faced. This practice of gratitude can foster a positive mindset and increase feelings of contentment.
3. **Comfort and support**: And times of distress, praying can be a source of comfort and support. Sharing your worries, fears, and hopes with God through prayer can provide solace and reassurance.
4. **Mindfulness and meditation**: Prayer can serve as a former mindfulness and meditation, helping individuals to center themselves, find inner peace, and cultivate a sense of calm amid life stresses and distractions.
5. **Strength and resilience**: Regular prayer can instill a sense of inner

strength, resilience, and faith in individuals. This can help them navigate challenges, setbacks, and uncertainties with the sense of hopes and determination.

6. **Community and connection**: For many people, prayer is a communal practice that connects them with others who share their faith and values. This sense of community can provide a support system and the feeling of belonging.

7. **Self-reflection and personal growth**: Through prayer, individuals can engage in self-reflection, examining their thoughts, beliefs, and actions. Introspection can lead to personal growth, insight, and a deeper understanding of oneself.

8. **Setting intentions and goals**: Praying can be a way to set intentions and goals, asking for guidance, wisdom, and strength and pursuing one's dreams and aspirations. This can foster motivation, clarity, and focus in achieving personal and spiritual growth.

9. **Healing and Wellness**: Some studies suggest that prayer can have positive effects on mental, emotional, and physical well-being. It may reduce stress, improve coping mechanisms, and promote overall health and healing.

10. **Spiritual connection and fulfillment**: For many individuals prayer is a way to nurture their spiritual life, deepen their faith, and cultivate a sense of meaning and purpose. It can provide a pathway to transcendence, enlightenment, and spiritual fulfillment.

It's important to note that the benefits of prayer may vary for each individual, depending on their beliefs, practices, and experiences. Whether one prays for guidance, gratitude, comfort, or connection, incorporating prayer into daily life can offer a sense of peace, purpose, and well-being.

CHAPTER 36

"The plan that will take you to your ultimate destination is the one you were created to carry out."

Your life purpose or ultimate destination is divinely ordained and guided by God. The unfolding of your life is a part of a greater plan or divine purpose that you were created to fulfill. Here are some ways in which this can shape your understanding of your life journey:

1. **Divine calling**: People are created by God for a specific purpose or mission. God's children should see themselves as instruments through which God works to bring about positive change, serve others, or fulfill a particular role in the world.

2. **Guidance and direction**: Those who are aware of a divine plan may seek guidance from God through prayer, meditation, and spiritual practices. They may look for signs, intuition, or inner guidance to discern the path that aligns with God's will for their life.

3. **Surrender and trust**: Trusting in God's plan can bring a sense of peace, surrender, and acceptance of the ups and downs of life. It can help individuals cope with uncertainty, setbacks, and challenges, knowing that they are ultimately held and guided by God or a higher power.

4. **Faith and resilience**: Believing in a divine plan can foster faith and resilience in the face of adversity. It can provide comfort, strength, and a hope in difficult times, knowing that God has a purpose for your struggles and will ultimately bring about good from them.

5. **Alignment with values and beliefs**: Following a divine plan often involves living in alignment with one's values, beliefs, and principles. It may involve acts of kindness, compassion, and justice that reflects God's love and purpose for the world.

6. **Co-creation with God**: Chosen individuals are shaping their destiny and fulfilling their purpose with God. They are a part of God's plan, using their gifts, talents, and opportunities to contribute to the greater good. This is called co-creation with God.

7. **Reflection and discernment:** Reflecting on one's life purpose and discerning God's plan may involve prayerful reflection, seeking wise counsel, listening to one's inner voice or intuition. It may require periods of silence, stillness, and inner listening to discern the path that aligns with God's calling.

God's plan for our life defines our divine purpose. Your ultimate destination is always the plan that you were created to carry out.

CHAPTER 37

"Be careful of what you speak. What you say materializes."

Words have a power and can manifest into reality. Here are some reasons why it's important to be careful with our words and mindful of what we speak:

1. **Law of attraction**: The law of attraction teaches that like attracts like, and that our thoughts and words have the power to create our reality. By speaking negative or limiting words, we may be unknowingly attracting more of that negativity into our lives. On the other hand, speaking positive, affirming words can help us manifest our desires and attract abundance and blessings.
2. **Words have energy**: Words are not just sounds that we utter; They carry energy and vibrations that can impact our own psyche as well as the world around us. Negative or hurtful words can create discord, conflict, and negativity, while positive and uplifting words can inspire, heal, and bring about positive changes.

3. **Self-fulfilling prophecy**: The words we speak can have a powerful influence on our beliefs, attitudes, and behaviors. When we repeatedly speak negative or self-defeating statements, we may internalize those messages and act in ways that align with those beliefs, creating a self-fulfilling prophecy. Conversely, speaking words of confidence, empowerment, and positivity can help us cultivate a mindset of success and abundance.

4. **Impact on others**: Our words not only affect ourselves but also have an impact on those around us. The things we say can uplift and inspire others or they can hurt and discourage them. Being mindful of the words we speak can help us cultivate harmonious relationships, build trust, and foster positive connections with others.

5. **Setting intentions**: By being intentional and thoughtful about the words we speak; we can set clear intentions for what we want to manifest in our lives. Affirmations, visualizations, and positive declarations can help us focus our energy and attention on our goals and dreams and align our words with our desires.

6. **Responsibility**: With the power of words comes a sense of responsibility. We are accountable for the impact of our words on ourselves and others. Being mindful of the language we use, the tone we adopt, and the messages we convey can help us cultivate greater awareness, empathy, and respect in our communication.

Being careful with our words and mindful what we speak is important because words have the power to shape our reality, influence our thoughts and actions, impact others, and set intentions for what we want to manifest in our lives. By speaking with awareness, intention, and positivity, we can align our words with our highest aspirations and create a more harmonious, empowered, and fulfilling existence.

CHAPTER 38

"Use your gifts and talents. Doors will open for you."

Using your gifts and talents can open doors for you in numerous ways, both personally and professionally. Here are some ways in which leveraging your strengths can lead to new opportunities and growth:

1. **Unique value proposition**: Each person has a unique set of gifts and talents that set them apart from others. By recognizing and utilizing your strengths, you can offer a unique value proposition that distinguishes you from your peers and competitors. This can attract opportunities, collaborations, and projects that align with your natural abilities.

2. **Passion and motivation**: When you are using your gifts and talents, you are likely engaged in activities that you are passionate about and enjoy. This passion can serve as a driving force that fuels your motivation, creativity, and resilience. This, in turn, can lead to greater levels of success and fulfillment in your endeavors.

3. **Personal growth**: Using your gifts and talents challenges you to continuously learn, grow, and develop your skills. By pushing yourself inside

of your comfort zone and honoring your abilities, you can cultivate a growth mindset and expand your potential. This personal growth can open doors to new opportunities and experiences that further enhance your abilities and potential.

4. **Networking and connections**: When you showcase your gifts and talents, you naturally attract like-minded individuals who appreciate and value your abilities. This can lead to networking opportunities, collaborations, and connections with others who may offer new insights, resources, and support that can propel your personal and personal growth.

5. **Recognition and opportunities**: When you excel in using your gifts and talents, you are more likely to receive recognition and acknowledgment for your abilities. This recognition can lead to opportunities for advancement, promotion, and leadership roles in your field. Employers, colleagues, and clients may seek out your expertise and skills, providing you with new avenues for growth and achievement.

6. **Increased confidence**: Using your gifts and talents can boost your self-esteem and confidence. As you achieve success and recognition in areas where you excel, you develop a stronger sense of self-belief and self-worth. This increased confidence can empower you to take on new challenges, pursue ambitious goals, and seize opportunities that may have previously seemed out of reach.

Leveraging your gifts and talents can open doors for you by providing a unique value proposition, fueling your passion and motivation, fostering personal growth, expanding your network, attracting recognition opportunities, and boosting your confidence. By embracing and utilizing your innate strengths, you can create new pathways for success, fulfillment, and growth in both your personal and professional life.

CHAPTER 39

"Be careful who you speak your plans to. It is better to keep them to yourself."

Everyone may not have your best interest at heart. Here are five reasons why you should keep your plans, goals, and dreams to yourself:

1. **Avoiding negative influence:** When you share your plans with others, you may encounter naysayers or individuals who doubt your abilities or feasibility of your goals. This negativity can undermine your confidence and motivation, making it harder for you to stay focused and committed to your plans. Keeping your plans private can shield them from external skepticism and allow you to pursue them with unwavering determination.

2. **Protecting your vision:** Sharing your plans with others can sometimes expose them to scrutiny, criticism, or unsolicited advice. This external feedback may hinder your ability to stay true to your vision and make decisions that align with your goals. By keeping your plans to yourself, you can protect your vision from outside influences and maintain a sense of clarity and purpose in pursuing your objectives.

3. **Maintaining focus:** Constantly talking about your plans and seeking

validation from others may divert your attention and energy away from actually taking concrete steps towards achieving them. By keeping your plans private, you can stay focused on your goals, prioritize your actions, and work diligently towards realizing your aspirations without distractions.

4. **Preventing disappointment:** Sometimes, sharing your plans with others can set high expectations that may not be met. If you face setbacks or challenges along the way, the pressure to live up to others' expectations can lead to disappointment or feelings of failure. Keeping your plans private allows you to work towards your goals at your own pace, without the pressure of meeting external benchmarks or timelines.

5. **Maintaining a competitive advantage:** In some competitive environments, sharing your plans with others could inadvertently give potential competitors insights into your strategies, goals, or upcoming projects. By keeping your plans confidential, you can maintain a competitive advantage and prevent others from capitalizing on your ideas or efforts.

There are times when you can benefit from sharing your goals with trusted individuals who can provide support, encouragement, and accountability. The decision to keep your plans private or to share them with others should always be well thought out and based on individual preferences, objectives, and circumstances.

CHAPTER 40

"Drinking much alcohol and continued smoking of any substance will drain your pockets."

Excess drinking, smoking, or substance abuse can have a significant impact on the individual's financial well-being in several ways:

1. **Cost of purchasing alcohol and cigarettes:** Regularly purchasing alcohol and cigarettes can be expensive, especially if consumed in large quantities. The cost of these substances can add up quickly and drain your finances, leaving you with less money for essential needs or savings.

2. **Healthcare costs:** Chronic alcohol consumption, smoking, and substance abuse can lead to a range of health issues, including cardiovascular disease, respiratory problems, liver damage and mental health disorders. The associated healthcare costs for treating these conditions can be substantial and place a financial burden on individuals, especially if they do not have adequate health insurance coverage.

3. **Reduced income potential:** Substance abuse can impact an individual's ability to perform effectively at work, leading to decreased productivity,

absenteeism, or even job loss period this can result in a loss of income, career setbacks, and limited opportunities for advancement or higher paying jobs.

4. **Legal consequences:** Engaging in excessive drinking, smoking, or substance abuse can increase the likelihood of legal issues such as DUI's, public intoxication, possession charges, or other criminal offices. The legal fees, fines, court costs, and potential loss of income due to legal troubles can further strain an individual's finances.

5. **Relationship and social cost:** Substance abuse can strain relationships with family, friends, and colleagues, leading to alienation, conflicts, and broken connections. Affected individuals may experience social isolation, loss of support networks, and strained personal or professional relationships which can have emotional and financial consequences.

6. **Impact on financial planning:** Continual spending on alcohol, cigarettes, or substances can hinder long term financial planning and goals, such as saving for retirement, buying a home, or investing in education period the money that could have been saved or invested for the future is instead being consumed by harmful habits, limiting financial stability and security.

It's essential to recognize the financial implications of excessive drinking, smoking, or substance abuse and consider seeking help or support to address these behaviors. Taking steps to reduce or eliminate these harmful habits can not only improve your financial situation but also lead to better health, relationships, and overall well-being.

CHAPTER 41

"One who loves pleasure and partying will become a poor individual."

An individual who loves pleasure and partying can potentially face financial difficulties and become poor for several reasons:

1. **Excessive spending:** People who prioritize pleasure in partying may tend to overspend on entertainment, dining out, drinks, clubbing, and other indulgences. Continuous spending on enjoyable activities without a budget or financial plan can quickly deplete one's savings and lead to accumulating debt.

2. **Impulse purchases:** Individuals who enjoy pleasure seeking activities may be more prone to making impulse purchases or non-essential items such as luxury goods, designer clothing, or the latest gadgets. These impulsive buying behaviors can result in wasteful spending and financial instability in the long run.

3. **Unpredictable income:** Jobs or careers that revolve around entertainment, nightlife, or partying may not always offer stable or reliable income. Income fluctuations, seasonal work, or a lack of job security can make it challenging to maintain a consistent financial standing,

particularly if one's lifestyle expenses are high.

4. **Lack of savings and emergency funds**. Prioritizing pleasure and immediate gratification over financial planning can lead to a lack of savings and emergency funds. Without proper savings for unexpected expenses, emergencies, or future needs, individuals may struggle to cope with financial setbacks and face financial insecurity.

5. **Health cost:** The lifestyle associated with excessive pleasure seeking and partying can have adverse effects on one's physical and mental health chronic partying, substance abuse, or overindulgence can lead to health problems that require medical treatment or therapy, resulting in additional healthcare costs and financial strain.

6. **Social and peer pressure:** People who enjoy partying and seeking pleasure may feel pressured to keep up with their social circle, friends, or influencers who promote A lavish lifestyle. Trying to maintain a certain image or keep pace other spending habits can lead to financial strain and the risk of overspending.

7. **Limited focus on long term goals:** People who prioritize immediate gratification and pleasure-seeking activities may neglect or overlook long term financial goals such as saving for retirement, investing in education, or building wealth. The lack of financial planning and foresight can hinder their ability to achieve financial stability and prosperity in the future.

Individuals who love pleasure and partying need to strike a balance between enjoying life experiences and maintaining financial responsibility. Developing good money management skills, setting financial goals, budgeting wisely, and prioritizing saving can help prevent financial hardships and support long term financial well-being.

CHAPTER 42

"Addictions bring about illnesses. Illnesses lead to death."

Addictions can lead to a range of illnesses that are often chronic and progressive, ultimately leading to death. Some ways in which addictions can contribute to illnesses that are life threatening include:

1. **Substance abuse:** Addictions to substances such as drugs, alcohol, or tobacco can cause a range of health problems that can be fatal. Substance abuse can lead to heart disease, liver cirrhosis, respiratory failure, and other organ damage, ultimately leading to death.
2. **Malnutrition:** Addictions can lead to poor nutrition and may result in malnutrition, which will inevitably weaken the immune system and cause individuals to be more susceptible to illnesses. Malnutrition can lead to a range of health issues, including organ failure and eventually death.
3. **Mental health disorders:** Addictions are often linked to mental health disorders such as depression, anxiety, and trauma. Untreated mental health disorders can have serious health consequences and may lead to increased risk of suicide or other fatal outcomes.
4. **Risky behaviors:** Addictions can lead to risky behaviors such as unprotected sex, driving under the influence, or engaging in violence. These

behaviors can increase the likelihood of accidents, injuries, and death.

5. **Overdose:** In cases of drug addiction, individuals may be at risk of overdose, which can be fatal. Overdose occurs when a person takes too much of A substance, leading to respiratory depression, coma, and death.

Addictions can have a profound impact on an individual's physical and mental health, leading to a range of illnesses that can ultimately result in death. Seeking treatment and support for addiction is essential to prevent these serious health consequences.

"Lay off the sweet treats."

There are several reasons why it's beneficial to reduce or limit the consumption of sweet treats in your diet:

1. **Weight gain:** Sweet treats are often high in calories, sugar, and unhealthy fats, which can contribute to weight gain and obesity. Consuming excess calories from sweet treats without burning them off through physical activity can lead to a caloric surplus, which is stored as fat in the body.

2. **Increased risk of chronic diseases**: Consuming too many sweet treats can increase your risk of developing chronic diseases such as type 2 diabetes, heart disease, and certain types of cancer. Excessive sugar intake

has been linked to inflammation, insulin resistance, and other metabolic issues that can contribute to the development of these conditions.

3. **Dental health:** Sweet treats high in sugar can promote tooth decay and cavities. Bacteria in the mouth feed on sugar and produce acids that erode tooth enamel, leading to dental problems and oral health issues.

4. **Energy crashes:** Eating sugary treats can cause a rapid spike in blood sugar levels, followed by a crash in energy levels. This can lead to feelings of fatigue, irritability, and cravings for more sugar, creating a cycle of energy highs and lows throughout the day.

5. **Nutrient deficiencies:** Sweet treats often lack essential nutrients such as vitamins, minerals, and fiber that are needed for Overall health and well-being. Consuming too many sugary snacks can displace nutritious foods in your diet, leading to nutrient deficiencies and poor health outcomes.

While it's OK to enjoy sweet treats and moderation as part of a balanced diet, it's important to be mindful of how much and how often you indulge in these foods. Choosing healthier alternatives such as fresh fruits, dark chocolate, or homemade treats with less sugar can help inspire sweet tooth without compromising your health.

CHAPTER 43

"There is power in your struggles."

The struggles that you face and the challenges that you overcome can ultimately make you stronger, more resilient, and more capable. While going through struggles may be tough and challenging, it can also be a transformative and empowering experience that helps you grow, learn, and develop as a person.

Struggles can push you out of your comfort zone, forcing you to confront your fears, limitations, and weaknesses. By overcoming these challenges, you can discover inner strength, carriage, and determination that you may not have realized you had period this can build of confidence, self-esteem, and sense of self-worth, empowering you to tackle future obstacles with greater resilience and optimism.

Struggles can also provide valuable opportunities for learning, personal growth, and self-discovery period going through difficult times can help you gain new insights, perspectives, and skills that can be applied to other areas of your life it can help you develop problem solving abilities, coping mechanisms, and emotional intelligence that can enhance your overall well-being and success.

Ultimately, embracing and learning from your struggles can help you become a more adaptable, resourceful, and empowered individual. It can teach you valuable life lessons, deepen your understanding of yourself and others, and cultivate a sense of gratitude and resilience that can serve you well in the face of future challenges. Just remember that it's OK to seek support, guidance, and assistance from others as you navigate your struggles and work towards personal growth and empowerment.

James 1:2-4

"Dear brothers and sisters, when trouble comes your way, let it be an opportunity for joy. Because when your faith is tested, your endurance has a chance to grow. So let it grow, for when your endurance is fully developed, you will be strong in character and ready for anything."

CHAPTER 44

LOVE

"Protect your heart. Do not compromise what you need in a relationship."

Protecting your heart and not compromising on your needs in a relationship is important for your emotional well-being and overall happiness. Here are a few reasons why it's crucial to prioritize yourself and your needs in a relationship:

1. **Self-worth and self-respect:** Setting boundaries and not compromising on your needs in a relationship communicates to your partner that you value yourself and your own well-being. It shows that you have self-respect and expect to be treated with love, respect, and understanding.

2. **Emotional health:** If you constantly compromise on your needs and suppress your true feelings and desires in a relationship, it can lead to feelings of resentment, frustration, and unhappiness. By honoring and protecting your heart, you are prioritizing your emotional health and well-being.

3. **Authenticity and honesty:** Being true to yourself and expressing your needs and desires openly and honestly in a relationship fosters authenticity and vulnerability. It allows you to build a strong emotional connection with your partner based on trust and mutual understanding.

4. **Sustainable and fulfilling relationships:** By standing up for your needs and not compromising on your values, you are setting the tone for a healthy and fulfilling relationship. It ensures that your relationship is built on mutual respect, communication, and compromise, rather than one sided sacrifices and compromises.

5. **Personal growth and fulfillment:** When you prioritize yourself and protect your heart in a relationship you are taking care of your own needs and well-being. This allows you to focus on personal growth, self-discovery, and emotional fulfillment, leading to a more fulfilling and satisfying life overall.

Remember that healthy relationships are based on communication, mutual respect, and compromise. It's important to communicate openly with your partner, set boundaries, and prioritize your own needs and well-being in order to build a strong and fulfilling relationship. Protecting your heart and not compromising on your knees is essential for creating a relationship that is based on love, respect, and understanding.

"Give ten percent of your wealth to the needy to unlock the blessings you seek."

Giving 10% of your wealth to the needy, also referred to as tithing, is a form of showing Godly love and obedience to the Word of God. Attached to the practice of giving money and resources to those in need and/or to and through your place of worship, is the spiritual and emotional benefit that comes from your generosity of love and selflessness. Here are a few reasons why tithing can unlock blessings and bring positive energy into your life:

1. **Gratitude and abundance mindset:** By tithing a portion of your wealth to those in need, you are practicing gratitude for the abundance and blessings in your own life. This act of giving helps shift your attention from what you don't have to what you do have, and it cultivates an abundance mindset that attracts more blessings and positive energy into your life.

2. **Empathy and compassion:** Giving to the needy fosters' empathy, compassion, and a sense of connection with others. It allows you to see beyond your own needs and desires and to recognize the struggles and challenges that others may be facing. This empathy and compassion can bring a sense of fulfillment and purpose to your life, opening you up to blessings and positive energy. It is wise to be a member of a place of worship that gives to those in need. This is a way to know that your tithe of love is falling on fruitful ground.

3. **Karma and spiritual principles:** The energy you put out into the world comes back to you in some form. You reap what you sow. By giving generously to those in need, you are putting positive energy and goodwill out into the universe, which can attract blessings and abundance back into your life.

4. **Community and enter connectedness:** Giving to the needy helps build a sense of community and interconnectedness with others. It creates a ripple effect of kindness and generosity that can bring blessings not only to those in need, but also to you and your community as a whole.

5. **Personal growth and fulfillment:** Tithing and giving to the needy can be a deeply fulfilling and rewarding experience. It allows you to make a positive impact on the lives of others, and can cultivate feelings of joy, gratitude, and fulfillment within yourself. This sense of fulfillment and personal growth can lead to greater blessings and abundance in all areas of your life.

Giving to the needy and tithing to your place of worship is a powerful practice that can unlock blessings, abundance, and positive energy in your life. It cultivates gratitude, empathy, and compassion, aligns you with spiritual principles, fosters community and interconnectedness, and promotes personal growth and fulfillment. By giving generously to those in need you are not only helping others but also inviting blessings and positive energy into your own life.

Malachi 3:8-12 discusses tithing in the Bible. It tells us that when we do not give 10% of our wealth as a tithe to the needy or our place of worship to give for us, it is robbing God. It goes on to tell us that if you do not do this you will not be blessed. Those who tithe 10%, at least, of their wealth are greatly blessed people. These are the people that see locked doors in their lives, unlock as they seek to walk through them.

"Keep your marriage/relationship pure. Going outside of it will bring poison."

Going outside of your relationship or marriage, commonly referred to as infidelity or cheating, can have detrimental effects on your relationship and bring poison to the union in several ways:

1. **Breakdown of trust:** Trust is the foundation of any healthy relationship. When one partner engages in infidelity, it breaches the trust that has been built between them. Trust is difficult to rebuild once it has been broken, and the betrayal of infidelity can leave lasting scars on the relationship.
2. **Communication breakdown:** Infidelity often leads to a breakdown in

communication between partners. The betrayed partner may struggle to express their feelings of hurt and betrayal, while the partner who cheated may feel guilt, shame, and fear of rejection. This lack of communication can further strain the relationship and make it difficult to address and resolve underlying issues.

3. **Emotional impact:** Infidelity can have a profound emotional impact on both partners. The betrayed partner may experience feelings of betrayal, anger, hurt, and low self-esteem. The partner who cheated may feel guilt, shame, and regret for their actions. These intense emotions can create a toxic and negative environment within the relationship.

4. **Erosion of intimacy:** Infidelity can erode the emotional and physical intimacy between partners. The betrayed partner may struggle to trust their partner and may withdraw emotionally and physically. The partner who cheated may also have difficulty reconnecting with their partner on a deep and intimate level. This erosion of intimacy can further strain the relationship and make it challenging to rebuild a strong and healthy connection.

5. **Long term consequences:** Infidelity can have long term consequences on a relationship, even if the couple chooses to stay together and work through the betrayal. The effects of infidelity can linger, causing ongoing emotional pain, resentment, and insecurity within the relationship. It can also create a cycle of distrust and insecurity that can be difficult to break.

Going outside of your relationship or marriage by engaging in infidelity can bring poison to that union by breaking down trust, communication, intimacy, and emotional well-being. Infidelity can create a toxic and negative environment that is challenging to overcome. It is essential to address and work through the underlying issues that lead to infidelity and seek professional help if needed to rebuild trust and strengthen the relationship.

CHAPTER 45

"Choose to show love. It confuses the enemy."

By choosing to love even those who may be considered enemies or adversaries, you are embodying the principles of forgiveness, compassion, and grace that are essential in the teachings of Jesus Christ. This act of loving your enemies can confuse the enemy in several ways:

1. **Disarming hostility:** When we choose to respond to hostility, anger, or hatred with love and kindness, it can disarm our enemies and disrupt the cycle of aggression and retaliation. This unexpected response of love can confuse and challenge their negative expectations, leading them to reconsider their attitudes and actions.

2. **Demonstrating God's love:** By choosing to love our enemies, we are demonstrating the transformative power of God's love and grace. This act of love can challenge the enemy's preconceptions about Christianity and inspire them to reconsider their own beliefs and behaviors.

3. **Overcoming evil with good:** Choosing to love our enemies goes against conventional wisdom and societal norms. It challenges the idea of re-

sponding to violence or hatred with more violence and instead advocates for responding with love and forgiveness. This act of choosing love over hate can confuse the enemy and challenge their worldview, potentially leading to a change of heart and reconciliation.

4. **Promoting reconciliation and peace:** By loving our enemies, we are actively seeking reconciliation and peace, rather than perpetuating conflict and division. This act of choosing love can sow the seeds of understanding, empathy, and forgiveness, ultimately leading to healing and restoration in relationships.

Choosing to love our enemies can confuse the enemy by challenging their attitudes, beliefs, and behaviors while embodying the transformative power of God's love and grace. It is a powerful and counter-cultural approach that has the potential to bring about healing, reconciliation, and peace in the face of conflict and hostility.

CHAPTER 46

"The light of evil doers will eventually go out. The light of a goodhearted person will grow brighter."

This statement is based on the biblical principle of the triumph of good over evil and the knowledge that righteousness will ultimately prevail. Light is used as a metaphor for goodness, truth, and God's presence, while darkness symbolizes evil, sin, and separation from God.

Those who engage in wickedness and wrongdoing will ultimately face judgement and consequences for their actions. In contrast, those who walk in righteousness, kindness, and love will experience blessings, growth, and the favor of God.

Proverbs 4:18 NLT says, "The way of the righteous is like the first gleam of dawn, which shines ever brighter until the full light of day." This verse emphasizes that the light of a righteous person will continue to shine brighter and illuminate the world with goodness and truth.

The message for Christians is to persevere in your faith, continue to do good, and trust in God's justice and mercy. By choosing to walk in the light of Christ and exemplifying his love and grace, you can shine brightly in a world filled with darkness and be a beacon of hope, healing, and redemption for others.

CHAPTER 47

"Heal your broken spirit quickly. If illness attacks you during this time, your body cannot withstand both."

Healing your broken spirit quickly is essential because your emotional and spiritual well-being are closely interconnected with your physical health. When you experience trauma, stress, or emotional pain, it can have a significant impact on your overall well-being and immune system. Research has shown that emotional distress can weaken the immune system, making the body more vulnerable to illness and diseases.

When illness attacks, the body is already in a state of vulnerability and stress from fighting off the sickness. If your spirit remains broken and you do not address it and heal the emotional wounds, it can further weaken your immune system and prolong recovery time. This can create a vicious cycle where physical illness exacerbates emotional distress, which in turn hinders the body's ability to heal.

Healing a broken spirit involves attending to emotional needs, seeking support from loved ones, practicing self-care, and finding healthy coping mechanisms to deal with stress and trauma. By addressing emotional wounds and nurturing our spiritual well-being, we can strengthen our resilience and immune system, helping the body better withstand the challenges of illness.

Ultimately, the mind, body, and spirit are interconnected, and healing one aspect can positively impact the others. Taking care of our emotional and spiritual health is just as important as caring for our physical well-being, especially during times of illness and vulnerability. By prioritizing holistic healing and nurturing your inner selves, you can support your body's healing process and promote overall wellness.

CHAPTER 48

"Beware of the person who woos you with a good meal."

There are people who will use gestures or acts of kindness, such as preparing a good meal, to manipulate or control the other person. The warning to "beware of the person who woos you with a good meal" is a reminder to be vigilant and cautious about someone's intentions, especially if they are using material things or acts of generosity to gain your trust or favor.

In some cases, a person may use gestures like cooking a good meal or showering you with gifts as a manipulation tactic to create a sense of obligation or indebtedness. They may use these actions to make you feel grateful, indebted, or obliged to them, thus creating a power dynamic in the relationship where they hold the upper hand.

Furthermore, using material gestures or acts of kindness as a primary means of winning someone over can be a sign of superficial or insincere intentions. True emotional connection and genuine care for someone go beyond material gifts or grand gestures. It is important to be cautious of individuals who rely solely on material displays of affection rather than building a meaningful and authentic connection based on mutual respect, trust, and understanding.

These words of wisdom serves as a reminder to pay attention to the intentions and dynamics of your relationships. It is essential to be mindful of potential manipulation or control tactics and prioritize relationships built on honesty, respect, and genuine **"When**

CHAPTER 49

you are righteous; when you are loyal and loving; your name will be honored."

By consistently demonstrating righteousness, loyalty, and love in their actions and interactions with others, they uphold their values and principles. People who see this behavior will naturally respect and honor them for their integrity and sincerity.

A person who is righteous, loyal, and loving often goes out of their way to support and help others in need. Their selfless acts of kindness and compassion can earn them a positive reputation and admiration from those they have helped.

Being loyal and loving in relationships fosters trust, respect, and deep connections with others. People value and honor individuals who are committed to nurturing and maintaining healthy, supportive relationships.

Someone who embodies righteousness, loyalty, and love is likely to contribute positively to their community or society. Their efforts to promote goodwill, justice, and compassion can leave a lasting impact and earn them the admiration and respect of others.

A person who consistently displays righteous, loyal, and loving behavior can serve as a role model for others. Their actions and values can inspire and influence those around them to strive for similar virtues, ultimately honoring their name by carrying on their legacy.

Living a life guided by righteousness, loyalty, and love can lead to a reputation of honor and respect. By embodying these virtues in their daily actions and interactions, an individual can cultivate a positive legacy that inspires admiration and reverence from those around them.

CHAPTER 50

"There is a class of people that curses it's father and does not bless it's mother." Proverbs 30:11

Knowing that there is a class of people who curse their father and do not bless their mother can serve as a cautionary reminder of the importance of honoring and respecting one's parents. Showing reverence and gratitude towards parents is considered a fundamental virtue.

Understanding the existence of individuals who do not show love and respect towards their parents can highlight the negative consequences of such behavior. It can emphasize the significance of familial relationships, the responsibility to care for and support one's family members, and the impact that neglecting or mistreating parents can have on familial dynamics and emotional well-being.

By acknowledging and reflecting on the behavior of those who curse their father and do not bless their mother, we can appreciate the value of honoring and cherishing our parents. It can serve as a reminder to express love and gratitude towards our parents, to treat them with kindness and respect, and to nurture positive relationships within our families. Ultimately, recognizing and understanding such behaviors can inspire us to prioritize familial bonds, strengthen family connections, and strive to be loving and respectful towards our parents and loved ones.

CHAPTER 51

"Apply your childhood teachings during your upbringing for a current situation."

Applying your childhood teachings to current situations can be beneficial for several reasons:

1. **Values and principles:** Childhood teachings often instill important values and principles that shape our moral compass and guide our behavior. By drawing on these teachings, we can make decisions that align with our core beliefs and values.
2. **Lessons learned:** Childhood experiences and teachings often provide valuable life lessons that can be applied to current challenges or situations; These lessons can help us navigate difficulties, make better choices, and learn from past mistakes.
3. **Emotional resilience:** Childhood teachings can help build emotional resilience and coping mechanisms that can be valuable in dealing with

stress, setbacks, and adversity. Drawing on these teachings can help us stay strong, positive, and focused during challenging times.

4. **Personal growth:** Reflecting on childhood teachings can also contribute to personal growth and self-awareness. By understanding how these teachings have shaped us, we can better understand ourselves, our motivations, and our behaviors, and make positive changes as needed.

Applying childhood teachings to current situations can provide a strong foundation for decision-making, problem-solving, and personal development.

CHAPTER 52

"Focus on the goal. Do not entertain distractions."

Focusing on the goal and not entertaining distractions is important for several reasons:

1. **Clarity and purpose:** Having a clear goal in mind helps us stay focused and purpose driven. By keeping our attention on the goal, we are more likely to make decisions and take actions that align with our objectives.
2. **Productivity and efficiency:** Distractions can derail our progress and hinder productivity. By staying focused on the goal, we can prioritize tasks, manage our time effectively, and work towards achieving tangible results.
3. **Motivation and determination:** Maintaining focus on the goal can boost motivation and drive. When we keep our eyes on the prize, we are more likely to stay motivated, persevere through challenges, and overcome obstacles along the way.
4. **Achievement and success:** Distractions can prevent us from reaching our full potential and accomplishing our goals. By eliminating distractions and staying committed to the goal, we increase our chances of achieving success and realizing our ambitions.

Focusing on the goal and avoiding distractions is key to maximizing productivity, staying motivated, and ultimately achieving success in both personal and professional endeavors.

CHAPTER 53

"It is time to seek after a career advancement."

Seeking career advancement is important for several reasons:

1. **Personal and professional growth:** Advancing in your career allows you to enhance your skills, knowledge, and capabilities. It provides opportunities for personal development and professional growth, helping you reach your full potential and achieve greater success.

2. **Increased earnings and financial stability:** Career advancement often comes with higher salaries, better benefits, and greater financial rewards. By pursuing opportunities for advancement, you can increase your earning potential and improve your financial stability.

3. **Job satisfaction and fulfillment:** Advancing in your career can lead to greater job satisfaction and fulfillment. Achieving new challenges, taking on more responsibilities, and progressing in your career can increase your sense of accomplishment and overall happiness in your work.

4. **Expanded opportunities and networking:** Advancing in your career opens up new opportunities for networking, mentorship, and professional connections. It can help you build a strong professional network, access new job prospects, and create valuable relationships that can

benefit your career in the long run.

5. **Recognition and esteem:** Career advancement often comes with increased recognition, respect, and esteem from colleagues, supervisors, and industry peers. It can boost your credibility, reputation, and professional standing, leading to greater opportunities for advancement the success.

Seeking career advancement is important for personal growth, financial stability, job satisfaction, networking opportunities, and professional recognition. By striving for career advancement, you can advance your skills, achieve your goals, and reach new heights in your professional life.

CHAPTER 54

"Is wise to take advantage of the doors that are opening for you."

Doors that open for you may not always be available, and it is important to seize the moment when opportunities present themselves. By taking advantage of open doors, you can capitalize on unique chances for growth, advancement, and success.

Embracing opportunities that come your way can lead to positive outcomes, such as career advancement, personal growth, and increased success. By stepping through open doors, you can further your goals, expand your horizons, and achieve new levels of achievement.

Taking advantage of open doors allows you to explore new possibilities, challenge yourself, and push beyond your comfort zone. By embracing opportunities for growth and advancement, you can reach your full potential and excel in your personal and professional life.

Embracing open doors can lead to new experiences, learning opportunities, and personal development. By stepping outside of your comfort zone and exploring new paths, you can expand your skills, knowledge, and capabilities, leading to personal and professional growth.

Taking advantage of open doors can create momentum and forward word progress in your life and career. By season opportunities, you can propel yourself toward your goals, overcome challenges, and move closer to achieving your aspirations.

Buy embracing opportunities as they arise, you can enhance your personal and professional growth, achieve success, and realize your dreams.

CHAPTER 55

"An honest business practice will multiply the bank account."

When you are honest in your business dealings, you build trust with your customers. Trust is an essential component of any successful business relationship, as it establishes credibility and reliability. Customers are more likely to do repeat business with a company that they trust, which can lead to increased sales and revenue.

Honesty and integrity are key factors in shaping our company's reputation. A good reputation can lead to positive word of mouth recommendations and referrals, which can attract new customers and expand your client base. Ultimately this can result in increased sales and business growth.

Honesty fosters customer loyalty and encourages repeat business. When customers trust that you will deliver on your promises and provide quality products or services, they are more likely to return to your business in the future. Repeat business is a key driver of revenue growth and can help to stabilize and grow your bank account over time.

Operating a business with honesty and integrity helps to ensure compliance with laws and regulations. By being transparent and truthful in your business practices, you reduce the risk of legal issues, penalties, and fines. Avoiding legal consequences can help you save money and protect your bottom line.

Honesty is a core value that contributes to the long-term success and sustainability of a business. Building a reputation for honesty and integrity can set your business apart from competitors and establish a strong foundation for growth and profitability. By cultivating a culture of honesty within your organization, you can create a positive, ethical business environment that attracts customers, employees, and partners, leading to sustained financial success.

Being honest in your business can multiply your bank account by building trust with customers, enhancing your reputation and referrals, fostering repeat business and customer loyalty, avoiding legal consequences, and promoting long term success and sustainability. Honesty is not only a moral imperative but also a strategic advantage that can drive financial growth and prosperity for your business.

CHAPTER 56

"Guard your mouth by thinking before you speak. Running off at the mouth will ruin you."

It is necessary to guard your mouth by thinking before you speak because words have the power to impact relationships, reputations, and opportunities. Running off at the mouth without consideration can lead to several negative consequences that can ruin you in various ways:

1. **Damage to relationships:** Speaking without thinking can result in saying things that are hurtful, offensive, or damaging to relationships. Words spoken and possibly in the heat of the moment can cause misunderstandings, conflicts, and irreparable damage to personal and professional relationships. Once words are spoken, they cannot be unsaid, and the damage to relationships may be difficult to repair.

2. **Harm to reputation:** Careless or thoughtless words can damage your reputation and credibility. In today's digital age, words spread quickly and can be easily captured and shared on social media and other platforms. Offensive or irresponsible remarks can tarnish your reputation, leading to loss of trust, respect, and credibility among peers, clients, and the public.

3. **Missed opportunities:** Speaking impossibly can result in missed opportunities in both personal and professional contexts. Ill-considered words

can alienate potential collaborators, clients, or employers, leading to missed opportunities for job projects, partnerships, or business deals. And effective communication can hinder your ability to convey your ideas, showcase your skills, or negotiate successfully.

4. **Legal consequences:** Speaking recklessly can have legal implications, leading to potential lawsuits, defamation claims, or other legal challenges. Slander, libel, or other forms of harmful speech carries art and legal action, financial penalties, and damage to your personal professional reputation.

5. **Personal and emotional consequences:** Running off at the mouth can also have personal and emotional consequences. Speaking impulsively can lead to regret, guilt, and shame, as well as strained relationships with loved ones. Unchecked words can also contribute to stress, anxiety, and negative emotions, affecting your overall well-being and mental health.

It is essential to guard your mouth by thinking before you speak to avoid the negative consequences of running off at the mouth. By practicing mindfulness, self-control, and effective communication, you can prevent harmful speech, protect relationships and reputation, seize opportunities, and maintain legal compliance. Thinking before you speak allows you to communicate thoughtfully and responsibly leading to positive outcomes and avoiding the pitfalls of reckless speech.

CHAPTER 57

"The lazy person gets nowhere. The diligent worker reaps in abundance."

Hard work, dedication, and perseverance are key factors to achieving success and abundance in life, while laziness and lack of effort will lead to stagnation and lack of progress.

The lazy person who does not put in the effort, time, and dedication required to achieve their goals will not see any significant progress or success. By procrastinating, avoiding responsibilities, and not taking action, they will not move forward in their personal or professional life. Ultimately their lack of diligence will result in missed opportunities, unfulfilled potential, and lack of growth and success.

On the other hand, the diligent worker who consistently puts in the effort, time, and dedication towards their goals will see positive results and abundance in various areas of their life. By taking action working hard and staying focused on their objectives, they are more likely to achieve success, reach their goals, and reap the rewards of their hard work period diligence and persistence are essential traits that lead to progress, achievements, and abundance.

This saying emphasizes the importance of hard work, consistency, and perseverance in achieving success and abundance in life. Those who are diligent and committed to their goals are more likely to succeed and prosper, while those who are lazy and lack motivation will struggle to make progress and achieve their full potential.

CHAPTER 58

"If you want to be wise, walk with wise people."

Associating with wise people can have a positive impact on your own wisdom and personal growth. Wise people have a wealth of knowledge, experience, and insight that they can share with you. By engaging in conversations, seeking advice, and observing their behavior, you can gain valuable insights, information, and wisdom that can help you broaden your perspective and deepen your understanding of various topics.

Wise people often demonstrate certain qualities, behaviors, and attitudes that contribute to their wisdom, such as critical thinking, emotional intelligence, and decision-making skills. By spending time with them and observing how they navigate challenges, make decisions, and handle relationships, you can learn by example and adopt some of their positive traits and habits.

Wise people can serve as mentors, advisers, and guides who can support and encourage you on your personal and professional journey. They can provide feedback, offer constructive criticism, and help you navigate difficult situations or decisions by drawing on their own experiences and wisdom.

Wise people may challenge your beliefs, assumptions, and perspectives, encouraging you to think critically, question your own ideas, and consider alternative viewpoints. By engaging in meaningful conversations and debates with them, you can expand your thinking, challenge your biases, and foster personal growth and self-improvement.

By surrounding yourself with individuals who demonstrate wisdom, integrity, and good judgment, you can cultivate your own wisdom and become a more thoughtful, insightful, and wise person over time.

CHAPTER 59

"It is good to gradually increase their wealth. Fast money dwindles quickly."

Gradually increasing wealth, as opposed to seeking fast money or sudden riches, office several advantages in terms of financial stability, long term success, and personal well-being. Gradual wealth accumulation allows you to build a solid foundation for your financial future by making consistent and sustainable progress over time period by focusing on steady growth and long-term financial planning, you are more likely to achieve lasting success and stability, rather than relying on risky or unsustainable shortcuts that may lead to financial setbacks.

Rapid wealth accumulation often involves taking high risk or making speculative investments that carry the potential for significant losses. By gradually increasing wealth through careful financial management, diversification, and prudent decision making, you can minimize the risk of financial warrant and protect your assets against unforeseen challenges or market downturns.

Building wealth gradually provides an opportunity to develop important financial skills, knowledge, and habits that contribute to long term financial success. By taking the time to learn about personal finance, investment strategies, and wealth management principles, you can make informed decisions, avoid common pitfalls, and build a solid financial future for yourself and your family.

The process of gradually increasing wealth can be as enriching and rewarding as the end goal itself. By setting achievable financial goals, creating a budget, and working towards incremental progress, you can cultivate discipline, patience, and resilience that contribute to personal growth, self-improvement, and a sense of accomplishment.

Gradually increasing wealth allows you to prioritize financial security, savings, and investments that support your long-term goals and provide a safety net for unexpected expenses or financial emergencies. By building wealth steadily and methodically, you can create a solid financial foundation that offers Peace of Mind, stability, and independence in the future.

By prioritizing steady progress, prudent decision making, and responsible financial management you can build a solid foundation for your financial future and achieve lasting success and prosperity over time.

CHAPTER 60

"Increase in wealth as you work towards your dreams and goals. Only talking about them will lead to poverty."

Working towards your dreams and goals rather than just talking about them is essential for achieving success and increasing wealth. Taking action towards your dreams and goals is what ultimately leads to progress, growth, and success. While talking about your aspirations can be inspiring and motivating, it is the actual work and effort you put in that will make a difference. By actively working towards your goals, you are more likely to see tangible results and move closer to achieving or desired outcomes.

Working towards your dreams and goals involves actively seeking out opportunities, being proactive, and taking calculated risk. By putting in the effort to pursue your aspirations, you open yourself up to new possibilities, connections, and experiences that can lead to wealth building opportunities, career advancement and personal growth.

Pursuing your dreams and goals often involves facing obstacles, setbacks, and challenges along the way. By taking action and working towards your objectives, you develop resilience, determination, and problem-solving skills that are crucial for overcoming adversity and achieving success. In contrast, merely talking about your dreams without taking action can lead to a sense of complacency and missed opportunities.

Consistent action towards your dreams and goals helps build momentum and progress over time period. Each step you take contributes to your growth, learning, and development, moving you closer to realizing your aspirations. By actively working towards your goals, you create a sense of momentum that propels you forward and brings you closer to achieving your desired outcomes.

By actively working towards your dreams and goals, you increase your chances of success, achievements, and financial prosperity. Whether your goals involve starting a business, advancing your career, investing in real estate, or pursuing other wealth-building opportunities, taking concrete steps towards your objectives can help you increase your earning potential, generate income, and build wealth over time.

By taking action, being proactive, and staying committed to your aspirations, you can bring your dreams into reality and achieve the level of success and financial prosperity you desire.

CHAPTER 61

"Welcome wise advice and seek counselors to help you succeed."

Welcoming advice from counselors or mentors can be invaluable in helping you succeed for several reasons:

1. **Gain valuable insights**: Counselors and mentors often have valuable insights, experience, and expertise that can help you gain a better understanding of your goals and challenges They can offer different perspectives, share knowledge, and provide guidance based on their own experiences, which can help you make more informed decisions and navigate obstacles more effectively.

2. **Receive personalized support**: Counselors and mentors can provide personalized support tailored to your unique needs, goals, and circum-stances. They can offer individualized guidance, encouragement, and feedback to help you identify areas for improvement, set realistic goals, and create a plan of action to achieve success.

3. **Accountability and motivation:** Having a counselor or mentor to support you can help keep you accountable and motivated as you work towards your goals. They can provide encouragement, keep you focused, and hold you accountable for your actions, helping you stay on track and maintain momentum even when faced with challenges of setbacks.

4. **Networking opportunities:** Counselors and mentors can also provide

valuable networking opportunities and connections that can help you expand your professional network, build relationships, and create new opportunities for growth and advancement. They may be able to introduce you to relevant contacts, resources, or opportunities that can further support your goals and increase your chances of success.

5. **Personal and professional development:** Working with a counselor or mentor can also contribute to your personal and professional development by helping you acquire new skills, knowledge, and strategies for success. They can offer guidance on persona growth, self-improvement, and skill-building, helping you develop the qualities and capabilities needed to achieve your goals and thrive in various aspects of your life.

By seeking guidance and support from experienced professionals, you can enhance your chances of success, overcome challenges more effectively, and achieve your goals more efficiently.

CHAPTER 62

LEADERSHIP

"You need to get clarification to help you understand the whole situation before making a decision."

Getting clarification helps to ensure that you have all the necessary information to make an informed decision. By understanding the whole situation, you can better evaluate the potential consequences of your decision and consider all relevant factors. This can help you make a more rational and well-thought-out choice, rather than acting impulsively or based on incomplete information.

Clarifying any uncertainties can help to avoid misunderstandings and miscommunication, ultimately leading to better outcomes.

Also by Vikki L. Pendleton

Knowledge Nuggets

Other books by Vikki L. Pendleton:
   BECOMING A WEALTHY BELIEVER
   BECOMING A WEALTHY BELIEVER PT. 2

Books coming soon:
   BECOMING A WEALTHY BELIEVER PT.3
   AFFIRMATIONS AND EXPLANATIONS
   Music, Music Videos, and Social Media for

Subscribers and Fans:
   WWW.YOUTUBE.COM/@DJJCHILL
   IG: @dj_jchill
   For Bookings:
   contactjchill@gmail.com
   vikki@VikkiLPendleton.com

All related websites:
   FeelizePublishingHouse.com
   FeelizeEntertainment.com
   VikkiLPendleton.com

www.ingramcontent.com/pod-product-compliance
Lightning Source LLC
Chambersburg PA
CBHW060542130626
46553CB00002B/861